LIVING WITH PURPOSE BIBLE STUDY

John

LIVING WITH PURPOSE BIBLE STUDY

John

A Gift from Guideposts

Thank you for your purchase! We want to express our gratitude for your support with a special gift just for you.

Dive into *Spirit Lifters*, a complimentary e-book that will fortify your faith, offering solace during challenging moments. Its 31 carefully selected scripture verses will soothe and uplift your soul.

Please use the QR code or go to **guideposts.org/spiritlifters** to download.

Living with Purpose Bible Study: John

Published by Guideposts
100 Reserve Road, Suite E200
Danbury, CT 06810
Guideposts.org

Copyright © 2025 by Guideposts. All rights reserved.

This book, or parts thereof, may not be reproduced, stored in a retrieval system, or transmitted in any form or by any means, electronic, mechanical, photocopying, recording, or otherwise, without the written permission of the publisher.

Cover design by Judy Ross
Interior design by Judy Ross
Cover photo by 52Ps.Studio/Getty Images
Typeset by Aptara, Inc.

ISBN 978-1-961251-34-2 (hardcover)
ISBN 978-1-961251-35-9 (softcover)
ISBN 978-1-961251-36-6 (ebook)

Printed and bound in the United States of America

CONTENTS

About Living with Purpose Bible Study 2

An Overview of John 5

LESSON 1: JOHN 1–3
Christ the Reconciler—as the Word of Grace 10

LESSON 2: JOHN 4–6
Christ the Reconciler—by Faith 40

LESSON 3: JOHN 7–9
Christ the Reconciler—in Freedom 66

LESSON 4: JOHN 10–12
Christ the Reconciler—in Truth 91

LESSON 5: JOHN 13–15
Christ the Reconciler—in Fellowship 117

LESSON 6: JOHN 16–17
Christ the Reconciler—in Unity 139

LESSON 7: JOHN 18–19
Christ the Reconciler—in Love 159

LESSON 8: JOHN 20–21
Christ the Reconciler—in Hope 180

APPENDIX
The Specific Miracles of Jesus in the Gospel of John 200
The "I Am" Statements in the Gospel of John 201
Map of Jesus's Travels in the Gospel of John 202
Jesus's Travels in the Gospel of John................................. 203
The Palestine of Jesus's Time 207
Map of the Jerusalem/Jericho Region 208
Map of the Region around the Sea of Galilee 209
A Harmony of the Gospels 210

Acknowledgments 219

A Note from the Editors 220

About Living with Purpose Bible Study

For as long as humankind has existed, we have pondered our place in the universe. Poets and preachers, philosophers and scientists alike have explored the topic for generations. Our busy modern lives leave little time for contemplation, and yet we move through our lives with nagging questions in the back of our minds: *Why am I here? What am I meant to do with my life?*

Fyodor Dostoyevsky wrote that the "mystery of human existence lies not in just staying alive, but in finding something to live for." You might wonder how living with purpose ties in with the Bible. That's because God's Word is a guidebook for life, and God Himself has a purpose—a unique mission—for and unique to you. Reading the Bible and seeking God through prayer are two of the main ways God speaks to people. And when we begin to seek God, when we pursue His truth, when we begin to live our lives in ways that reflect His love back to others, we begin to find that purpose. Finding our purpose is not a destination; it is a journey we'll travel until we leave this earth behind and go to our heavenly Father.

Most of us know something about the Bible. We might be able to quote verses that we memorized as kids. Many of us have read parts of it, have learned about it in Sunday school both as children and adults. But not as many of us *know* the Bible, and that is where this Bible study comes in.

"Bible study" is a term that can elicit a variety of responses. For some people, the feeling that comes is a daunting sense of intimidation, even fear, because we worry that the Bible will somehow find us wanting, less than, rejected. Maybe we've heard preachers wielding the Bible as a weapon, using it as a measuring rod and a dividing line that separates "us" from "them."

Guideposts' *Living with Purpose Bible Study* addresses these questions and concerns with a hope-filled, welcoming, inclusive voice, like the one you've grown to know and love from Guideposts' devotional books, story collections, magazines, and website.

Best of all, you'll discover that the writers of *Living with Purpose Bible Study* are experts not only in the depth of their Bible knowledge but also in sharing that knowledge in such a welcoming, winning way that you can't help but be drawn in.

The writers come alongside you as trusted friends, guiding you through each volume in that warm, inviting manner that only Guideposts could bring you.

Each volume in the study draws from five trusted translations of the Bible: the New International Version, New American Standard Bible, the Amplified Version, the English Standard Version, and the King James Version of the Bible. We encourage you to keep your favorite Bible translation on hand as you read each study chapter. The Bible passages you read act as the foundation from which the study writer's insights, information, and inspiration flow. You can read along with the writers as each chapter unfolds, or you can read all of the passages or verses included in the chapter prior to reading it. It's up to you; you can use the method that works best for you.

In addition, you'll find two distinct features to enhance your experience: "A Closer Look" entries bring context by presenting historical, geographical, or cultural information, and "Inspiration from the Gospel of John" entries demonstrate the spiritual insights people like you have gained from their knowledge of the biblical text. We've also provided lined writing spaces at the end of each lesson for you to jot down your own thoughts, questions, discoveries, and *aha* moments that happen as you read and study.

A final note: Before you read each chapter, we encourage you to pray, asking that God will open your eyes and heart to what He has to say. Our prayer for you is that you find a new or renewed sense of purpose and grow closer to God as you deepen your understanding of God's Word by enjoying this *Living with Purpose Bible Study*.

—*The Editors of Guideposts*

An Overview of John

"John, perceiving that what had reference to the bodily things of Jesus's ministry had been sufficiently related, and encouraged by his friends, and inspired by the Holy Spirit, wrote a spiritual gospel."

This perceptive comment written in the third century by Clement of Alexandria, one of the most profound scholars in the Early Church, will most certainly come alive for us as we study the Gospel of John. For countless millions of Christians, this "spiritual Gospel" has been, and is, the most loved book in our Bible.

The Gospel of John states its purpose, not at the beginning of the book, as one might expect, but near the end. The writer states that it was written that we might believe "that Jesus is the Messiah, the Son of God, and that by believing you may have life in his name" (20:31, NIV). John's purpose statement becomes ours when we believe in Jesus and gain life, both now and forever, through Him.

It is clear that the writer of this Gospel was intimately familiar with not only Jesus's words but also His thoughts. As in no other place, we sense the thinking and the heart of Jesus as John pulls aside the curtain and helps us come to grips with His meaning.

The Early Church leaders, such as Clement, Augustine, and Origen, passed along to us through history the understanding that this Gospel was written at Ephesus by the Apostle John.

Irenaeus, the Bishop of Lyons circa AD 180, who had known the aged Polycarp, a convert and colleague of John, wrote, "John, the disciple of the Lord, who leaned on His breast, himself issued the Gospel while dwelling in Ephesus." It is clear that these Early Church leaders believed and accepted without question that this John was one of Jesus's chosen twelve, and the one identified six times in the Gospel as "the disciple whom Jesus loves."

As with the John who is credited as the author of the book of Revelation, Bible scholars debate the specific identity of the author of John's Gospel, suggesting that the book's skilled use of Greek puts it outside the capabilities of a Galilean fisherman. There is disagreement among modern Bible experts as to whether all of the Gospel actually came from John's pen, whether an unknown scribe recorded and organized the spoken testimony of the Apostle John, or whether parts of it were collected and compiled by a different individual or multiple individuals.

These debates notwithstanding, the Early Church fathers, who lived only a few generations after Jesus's earthly ministry, seemed quite certain that it originated from the heart and reflections of the Apostle John himself.

The Gospel may have been written as early as AD 70, but most scholars think it was more likely AD 85–90. In any case, it existed in its final form by AD 90–110. We know it was being circulated in Egypt by AD 130 because of a papyrus fragment of the Gospel that was found there in 1920. Allowing a generation for it to travel means that the Gospel was written by at least AD 100—a time close enough to the events in the earthly life of Jesus to assure the book's historical accuracy, and far enough removed to avoid emotional embellishments.

None of the writers of the synoptic Gospels—Matthew, Mark, and Luke—attempted to record a strictly biographical or historical account of Jesus' life and ministry. This is equally true, if not more so, of this fourth Gospel. And while there are similarities between this Gospel and the other three, there are also significant differences.

John selected materials from the life and teachings of Jesus to develop for his Greek readers a presentation of Christ as God's Son and the Savior of the world. While not written chronologically, which seems to be more the case in the Synoptics, this Gospel, like the others, is basically telling the Jesus story.

John omits some of the familiar stories found in the Synoptics, such as Jesus's birth, baptism, temptation, transfiguration, institution of the Lord's Supper, and agony in the garden. Missing also are the lively and graphic parables that are found in the other Gospels. He does, however, relate a number of additional accounts—not found in the Synoptic Gospels—such as the conversation between Nicodemus and Jesus, which gives us the gospel in a nutshell (3:16); His meeting with the Samaritan woman at the well in Samaria; the raising of Lazarus; the foot-washing; the trial before Annas; and several post-Resurrection appearances.

John's primary divergence is in arrangement—for example, placing the cleansing of the temple at the beginning of Jesus's ministry, for reasons we can only speculate about.

John's theological approach begins with the preexistent Christ being incarnate in Jesus of Nazareth. He treats Jesus's miracles as "signs" that identify Him as the Son of God. He presents the "King" rather than the Kingdom. Though in the Synoptics the "kingdom of God" is a common theme, in John's Gospel, the Kingdom is interpreted in terms of the larger theme of fellowship with God (3:3–5; 18:36). John writes of the new life that Christ came to bring us. And this life is presented as a faith relationship with the Father through Christ, mediated to us by the Spirit of God (chapters 3, 6, 10, 15, 16, 17).

Yet despite the differences between John and the Synoptic Gospels, John's theology is not other than—different from—the one heard and recorded by the other disciples. In Matthew 11:27 Jesus said, "All things have been handed over to Me by My Father; and no one knows the Son except the Father; nor does anyone know the Father except the Son, and anyone to whom the Son determines to reveal Him" (NASB). Similarly, John wrote, "No one has seen God at any time; God the only Son, who is in the arms of the Father, He has explained Him" (1:18, NASB). Nine-tenths of the material in John is not in the other Gospels—but the overarching message and purposes of all four Gospels are the same.

John's Gospel is especially rich in identifying Jesus as the Son of God; in discussing the Holy Spirit, with five great passages on His person and work; in sharing the upper-room discourses, including the marvelous high-priestly prayer; and in reviewing Resurrection appearances to convince the skeptical disciples.

It has been said that John's Gospel is the earliest form of preaching the gospel—of telling the Jesus story. John holds the Jesus of history and the Christ of faith together as one and the same. John's Gospel interprets Jesus for Jew and Gentile alike as the Redeemer who came to reconcile us to God. Christ is the One in whom God is manifested, "reconciling the world unto himself" (2 Corinthians 5:19, KJV). John presents his book as a missionary tract, revealing not merely the gospel that Jesus *taught* but that Jesus Himself is the Good News—because He is the one who reconciles us to the Father.

How blessed we are to have this unique fourth Gospel as the Spirit's gift to His church. May we find purpose and meaning as these words inspire and strengthen us to make Jesus the central, prescriptive, and determining force in our lives.

LESSON 1: JOHN 1–3

Christ the Reconciler— as the Word of Grace

Heavenly Father, help me to hide Your Word in my heart that I might not sin against You. AMEN.

The message of grace is simply that "God was in Christ, reconciling the world unto himself" (2 Corinthians 5:19, KJV). God took the initiative; He moved to us, overcoming our rebellion and estrangement by His love and reconciliation. In Jesus Christ we come to an understanding of God, and we come into fellowship with God (John 1:12). John writes, "For the law was given by Moses, but grace and truth came by Jesus Christ" (1:17, KJV). John introduces us to the reconciling work of Christ.

Jesus came "that they may have life, and have it to the full" (10:10, NIV). In His prayer He said, "And this is eternal life, that they know you, the only true God, and Jesus Christ whom you have sent" (17:3, ESV). In all of this we see that the Gospel of John was written to present Jesus as the eternal Son of God, the One in whom we know the Father and in whom we are reconciled to the Father. Jesus said, "I am the way, and the truth, and the life; no one comes to the Father except through Me" (14:6, NASB).

The Word—as the Light of Life

John's Gospel opens with a poetic prologue (1:1–18), which is one of the most profound and beautiful statements about Christ in Scripture. Here Jesus is presented as the eternal *Logos* (Word), who was with the Father from eternity—for all time past and future—and He identified with the Father as God. There are three affirmations of the Word made in this part of our Scripture lesson: First, "The Word was God" (1:1–2); second, the Word created all things (1:3–10); and third, the Word took human form and dwelled among us (1:11–18). This emphasis is spelled out graphically and poetically for us in Proverbs 8:22–31. These verses present a fascinating Old Testament parallel and foreshadowing to John's prologue. You will find it helpful to turn to these verses and read them before continuing with this part of our study.

The mystery of the Incarnation is that God took human form to fully reveal Himself to us. Throughout the Old Testament, from stories of God's acts and discourses, we learn many profound things about Him. Now, in Jesus of Nazareth, this God of the Old Testament comes to us; we actually meet Him.

For God to become incarnate in human form without being sinful means that humanness and sinfulness are not synonymous (1:14). Instead, sinfulness is a perversion of humanness. From this we come to see that redemption is in some way the correction of the perversion; it is the re-creation of what is truly human! And since sinfulness is rebellion against God, salvation through Jesus Christ is our reconciliation to God, our becoming children of God (1:11–12).

The famed reformer Martin Luther spoke of the three forms of the Word of God: (1) the eternal Word, the Christ; (2) the written Word, the Scripture; and (3) the preached Word, the witness in action. In the first eighteen verses of this Gospel all three forms are expressed. Jesus is the eternal Christ. John the Baptist is introduced as the prophetic witness (1:6–8). And the preaching of the Word is expressed in the comments of John the Baptist (1:15) and of John the writer (1:16–18).

The concluding words of this prologue to the Gospel express the fact that the living Word, the only begotten Son, came to make God known to us. We now have a God who is not an impersonal, abstract idea but a God with a face. He is not "Someone out there"; He is here *with* us. In Jesus we can now address God as *Abba*, as Father, or in a more familiar sense, Daddy.

These first eighteen verses of the Gospel have been referred to by some as a possible hymn in the Early Church. Whether this was so or not, the life of fellowship with God is a life of joy and celebration. Singing His praise is a meaningful part of our worship—an identification of believers with one another in the joy of reconciliation. And this reconciliation is in Jesus, the Word of God's grace. As John's introduction of his Gospel, these verses may be seen in three divisions: (1) the Word *as* the Incarnation (verses 1–2, 14); (2) the world *and* the Incarnation (verses 3–4, 10); and the witness *to* the Incarnation (verses 6–7, 15–17).

For us, to know Jesus is to know God, and to receive Jesus is to be reconciled to God. As Paul expressed this, "He made Christ who knew no sin to [judicially] be sin on our behalf, so that in Him we would become the righteousness of God [that is, we would be made acceptable to Him and placed in a right relationship with Him by His gracious lovingkindness]" (2 Corinthians 5:21, AMP). In other words, the sinless Jesus assumed our sin so that we would be righteous in God's sight.

The Word—as the Lamb of God

The story of Jesus is rooted in the acts of history. It is not a religious myth. It is the account of God's acts among people in Jesus Christ. For centuries, the divine revelation—the Scriptures—had predicted the coming of the Christ.

Each of the four Gospels presents John the Baptist, the wilderness preacher, as the herald of the King. John's message of repentance was more than a call to personal piety; it was a call for people to prepare for the coming of the Kingdom, for the arrival of the Messiah. His message was so clear and his ministry so successful that vast crowds of people were reached and moved. And the leaders of the Jewish religious bureaucracy came to inquire of John whether he was the Christ, the Messiah. This not only speaks of respect for John but tells us of the general expectation of the coming Messiah.

A study of John the Baptist as presented in the Gospels reveals his unique character. Yet Jesus said the lowliest person in the new Kingdom—His new fellowship—has greater privilege than had John. Of John the Baptist himself we are shown that he had (1) a proper estimation of himself (1:19–26); (2) a spirit of humility (3:30); (3) a spiritual radiance (5:35); (4) a witness of righteousness (Mark 6:20); and (5) a clear witness of the Christ (10:41). In speaking of Jesus, John the Baptist said that he wasn't fit to unloose His sandals (1:27).

There are many names used to describe Jesus in John's Gospel, but one of the more expressive is this early statement from John the Baptist, "Behold, the Lamb of God, who takes away the sin of the world!" (1:29, ESV). These words are reminiscent of Abraham's words to Isaac, "God himself will provide the lamb for the burnt offering" (Genesis 22:8, NIV), and of the deliverance of Israel from Egypt with the sacrifice of the lamb for the Passover (Exodus 12:1). They also remind us of Isaiah's words, "He was led like a lamb to the slaughter, and as a sheep before its shearers is silent, so he did not open his mouth" (Isaiah 53:7, NIV). Jesus is the lamb of God, ". . . our passover is sacrificed for us" (1 Corinthians 5:7, KJV). In addition to the pictures of the Paschal (Passover) lamb and of the suffering servant, the Jewish community looked for an apocalyptic lamb in the final judgment.

It is clear that John, in writing his Gospel, is telling Jesus's story with a theological interest. He is not simply giving a biography of the life of Christ, but he is lifting from the life of Jesus and arranging—in his carefully chosen, preferred order of illustration—a selection of events and teachings that communicates the Good News of God's new fellowship.

Having introduced Jesus as the eternal Word of God, he now presents Jesus as the atoning reconciler of people to God.

The redemptive act of atonement is (1) to take away our sin; (2) to pay the price of forgiveness; and (3) to express the fullness of God's love.

The witness of John the Baptist presented Jesus as the one who fulfills God's promise as it was given through the Old Testament prophets. John also bears witness to the Word from God that "He upon whom you see the Spirit descending and remaining upon Him, this is the One who baptizes in the Holy Spirit" (1:33, NASB). John can therefore say, "This is the Son of God" (1:34, KJV). John's announcement is that above all, Jesus baptizes with the Spirit. He gives to His disciples of all time the gift of God's inner presence!

It is important to note that John the Baptist described his own ministry as focused on Christ, saying that the sole purpose of his preaching and baptizing was that the Christ "should be made manifest," that is, that He should be made known to the people (1:31). And making Jesus known is the test of all true service. All that we do as witnesses, as worship leaders, as workers in social service, should point to Jesus.

A story is told of Leonardo da Vinci, the early sixteenth-century artist who painted the Last Supper scene on a dining room wall of a monastery in Milan. As a visitor stood viewing the finished work, he commented on the realism of several goblets on the table, exclaiming that they were so realistic he felt as though he could reach out and pick them up. Upon hearing those words, the artist quickly grabbed a brush and painted out the goblets. Pointing to Jesus he said, "It's His face! His face, that I want you to see."

The Word—the Master

We are now introduced to four men who became disciples of Jesus (1:35–51). A disciple is one who learns from and identifies with the Master. And the Christian life is discipleship of Jesus. A sixteenth-century Anabaptist, Hans Denck, said, "No one knows Christ truly unless he follows Him daily in life." Salvation is a relationship with Jesus, for in Him we are reconciled to God.

This part of our Scripture lesson is opened with a second affirmation by John that Jesus is the "Lamb of God" (1:29, 36). It was this identification of Jesus that led two of John the Baptist's disciples to leave him and follow Jesus. John always pointed attention away from himself to Jesus as the Messiah, the Christ.

In leaving John the Baptist and following Jesus, these two men exhibited the supreme act of faith. Their attention was turned from the religion to which John had introduced them to the Person of Jesus, whom they referred to as Master (1:38).

The directness of Jesus in His relationships with people is always interesting. When He realized the two men were following Him, He turned and asked what they wanted. They countered by asking where He lived—an indication that they wanted to be with Him. And in response Jesus said, "Come and see" (1:39, KJV). In reality, this was an invitation not just to "see" or to talk but to learn from Him. And their response was to follow Him and live with Him.

This is the essence of true discipleship—to be with Jesus. Their allegiance was transferred from John to Jesus. A faith that saves is faith in the Savior; not faith in religion or in morality, but faith in Christ. As Paul wrote later, he had to discover that the righteousness of the law could only reconcile him with the law, but the righteousness of God in Christ reconciled him with God! (Philippians 3:9).

In this part of our lesson we see the Master as He walks into people's lives and calls them to be His disciples. And He does this today as He calls us to follow Him, to confess Him as Lord, and to become His servants.

One of the two disciples who turned to Jesus is identified as Andrew (1:40). Andrew, with the conviction that Jesus was actually the Christ, went first and found his brother Simon and brought him to Jesus (1:41–42). What a marvelous example we have in Andrew's first act of bringing his brother to Jesus. And in John's Gospel there are two other references to Andrew bringing people to Jesus: the boy with his lunch (6:8–9) and the Greeks who came to see Jesus (12:22). We need to join the fellowship of Andrew—bringing people to Jesus. This is our model today for sharing the Good News of Jesus. And we also need to recognize that salvation is not for individualistic piety but for community.

When the Master makes disciples of people, it is not at a shallow level but with a full understanding of their person. In fact, His understanding of us enhances our own self-awareness. In our search for identity, Jesus, by His call, gives us our identity.

This truth is illustrated by Jesus's meeting with Simon when He gave him a new name. Jesus changed Simon's name to Cephas, which in Aramaic means "a rock." Peter is the Greek translation of the same word. Jesus may well have given him the nickname "Rocky" as a prophecy of his future strength. Although it took Peter a while to manifest his new identity, Jesus gave it to him at that moment. How wonderful it is that Jesus sees possibilities in us, as He did in Peter, that exceed anything we might imagine!

The scene now seems to shift from southern Palestine to the north in Galilee (1:43). Here, possibly in Cana, Jesus met Philip, whose home was in Bethsaida. To Philip He said, "Follow me," and it is apparent that Philip not only accepted Jesus's call, but he went right out and found a friend, Nathanael, and told him he had found the Messiah and that He was Jesus of Nazareth. Nathanael's derisive response, "Can anything good come out of Nazareth?" (1:46, ESV), was answered by Philip in the best possible way: "Come and see." The dialogue between Jesus and Nathanael is intriguing (1:47–51). Jesus began by complimenting him on his integrity and faithfulness to his Hebrew heritage. And from there Jesus led Nathanael to the point that he recognized the One from Nazareth as "the Son of God . . . the king of Israel" (1:49, KJV).

The interchange between Jesus and Nathanael ties the disclosure of the Christ, the Messiah, to Old Testament prophecies. It is likely that Jesus's comment about seeing Nathanael "under the fig tree" (1:48, ESV) is a reference to the Messianic time spoken of so poetically by the prophet Micah (4:3–4) when everyone could study Scripture under his own vine and fig tree. Possibly Nathanael had been doing just that prior to this dramatic meeting. At any rate, he was convinced as to who Jesus was and used two specific Messianic titles in addressing Him—Son of God and King of Israel (1:49).

Jesus is indeed the Son of God—our Lord. This is the declaration of saving faith with which all believers are identified. In the days when John wrote this Gospel, early Christians were undergoing intense persecution because people within the Roman Empire were commanded to worship the emperor. Each person was asked to declare that Caesar was lord. The Christian response was, "Jesus is Lord, not Caesar." For them, no temporal authority could replace their commitment to Jesus Christ. In similar fashion, Christians in the twenty-first century must stand firm in *our* commitment to the Lordship of Christ and not succumb to the temptation in our social and political realms to render to "the caesars" of our time. We are to render to Caesar only what is Caesar's because we must render to God all that is His (Matthew 22:21).

The Word—as Creative Act of God

Our Scriptures give us a creation theology. The high points in Scripture regarding creation are Genesis 1–2, John 1, Colossians 1, and Hebrews 1. We learn from these Scriptures that (1) the Creator is distinct from His creation; (2) the Creator made a good world; (3) God created us in the *imago Dei* (the image of God); and (4) sin is an intrusion into the world, a perversion of the good.

We learn also that the Christ was promised to come and to correct the perversion of sin and restore our fellowship with God. Paul wrote that we are "predestined to become conformed to the image of His Son" (Romans 8:29, NASB). This is not a "creation science" but a creation theology, for science can study the creation but it cannot discover the Creator except through the Creator's own self-disclosure. In reality, the created order, which we know as our universe, is only a "mute witness" of what is interpreted by our Scriptures.

Now, in this part of our Scripture lesson (2:1–11) we are introduced to the creative power of the Son of God. The first verse of John's Gospel identified the Word as "with God, and the Word was God" (KJV). Next, in verses 2 and 3 we learned that the Word was with God in the beginning, and "all things were made by him" (KJV).

John now introduces us to the first of seven of Jesus's miracles—signs—that he gives us in his Gospel: the act of turning water into wine. This is the "sign" of the creative Word personified in Jesus of Nazareth. We see Him here as the Creator Lord, and His act discloses His glory to the disciples, and from this early stage the disciples begin to see Jesus as their Messiah (2:11). John's reference to Jesus's glory here reminds us of his earlier witness: "We beheld his glory, the glory as of the only begotten of the Father" (1:14, KJV). This sign shows us the plenteous supply of God's grace. It reminds us of Elijah's miracle in supplying the widow with meal and oil (1 Kings 17:1–16). It is also reminiscent of Elisha's miracles, when he supplied oil for a widow and her sons (2 Kings 4:1–7) and loaves for the people (2 Kings 4:42–44).

It is no surprise that many wedding sermons have been preached from these verses, for Jesus graced the wedding at Cana with His presence. Marriage is to be sanctified by God's presence and purpose. And two people in love should enter marriage in faith and integrity, knowing that the spiritual vitality for their success is the presence of the Christ—in Him they are never alone. And the dynamic of Christian community is in our relating to one another in and through Christ. This means that we do not relate without Him lest we intimidate, manipulate, dominate, or coerce one another. Instead we relate to others in freedom through Him.

There is a tradition (a belief or understanding that has been passed on from the earlier days of the church) that the wedding that day in Cana may have been in the family of Zebedee, and that Zebedee's wife, Salome, was a sister to Mary, the mother of Jesus. This may explain Mary's special feeling of concern over the wine shortage and why she came to Jesus for help. It isn't likely ahead of time that Mary knew what Jesus would do, but it is obvious that she trusted Him.

Jesus's response to His mother in verse 4 sounds abrupt, but it could have just as well been translated, "Woman, what have you and I to do with that?" (The original word translated "woman" was really a title of respect, although to us, it, too, sounds abrupt.) Jesus then added, "My hour has not yet come" (2:4, ESV), and this could mean that it wasn't yet time for Him to act, either to show His glory or to not intervene until the situation actually became hopeless.

But we read next, in verses 6–8, that Jesus did act by instructing the servants to fill six large stone jars to the brim with water. He then told them to "draw some out now" (NASB) from the jars and take the contents—the water that had become wine—to the "master of the banquet" (2:8, NIV).

The reaction of the "headwaiter" (verse 8, NASB) in the story is highly significant as he discovered that this wine was so much better than the wine that had been served earlier (2:9–10), for he asked the bridegroom why he had saved the best for the last.

There are several lessons for us in this remarkable story. First, it would have been terribly embarrassing for a Jewish host to have run out of wine before the wedding celebration was over. But Jesus, always sensitive to the feelings and needs of people, stepped in and prevented that embarrassment through His gracious act.

It is significant that Jesus is a part of this festive occasion honoring the marriage of two friends. Not only was His presence there a blessing to the marriage, but apparently here, as in many later occasions, He was enjoying Himself with people. He evidently mixed and mingled well.

But of primary importance, through Jesus's creative act we have a magnificent symbol of the arrival of what we might call the new wine of God's new Kingdom—the new fellowship of believers in Jesus Christ. It was a time of celebration because in Jesus a new quality has come into our lives (Mark 7:1–24), which stands in stark contrast to the cold and formal rule-following that was taught and practiced by the Pharisees.

Our Lord is the Creator; He is active in our lives. And we recognize Him as creating His church in every culture and time, meeting human needs with creative acts that glorify God the Father.

The evidence of His work of creation is all around us. As we view God's magnificent creation, we know that Someone was at work here. And as we meet Jesus, we now know what the Creator is like. God is like Jesus, active in His love.

The Word—as the Messiah

In this next scene we find Jesus and His disciples in Jerusalem to celebrate the Passover as John describes the cleansing of the temple court as an expression of His Messianic authority (2:12–17). God's house is to be a center of worship for everyone, but the impiety and crass materialism of the Jewish religious leaders had led to the cluttering of the court of the Gentiles with their business traffic so that the Gentiles could not come to worship. The prophet Malachi predicted, "'The Lord you are seeking will come to his temple; the messenger of the covenant, whom you desire, will come,' says the LORD Almighty. But who can endure the day of his coming? Who can stand when he appears? For he will be like a refiner's fire or a launderer's soap. He will sit as a refiner and purifier of silver; he will purify the Levites" (Malachi 3:1–3, NIV). We see in this that the judgment of God hangs over the old order, for the new has come!

In the other Gospels, the cleansing of the temple is said to have occurred in the closing days of Jesus's life. Either there were several occasions of cleansing the temple, or John selected this account for an early presentation of the authority of Jesus. John in his Gospel chose to emphasize the cleansing of the temple and the zeal for the house of God that motivated Jesus. In Mark's Gospel we have the words "Is it not written, 'My house shall be called a house of prayer for all the nations'?" (Mark 11:17, ESV) as an expression of Jesus's concern for all.

This event is used by some to argue that Jesus resorted to violence, thereby justifying the use of violence in human conflict. But this would contradict Jesus's strategy of love in His Sermon on the Mount, for He taught that we should turn the other cheek.

It would appear that Jesus made the whip to drive out the sheep and the oxen. He overturned the tables of the money changers and verbally denounced those who were guilty of misusing the temple. But there is no proof that He laid the whip on any person. It is true from what John has written that Jesus was angry, but His anger was directed at a system that permitted worshippers to be taken advantage of and the house of God to be desecrated. In other words, it is unlikely that Jesus's anger was provoked by people. Actually, anger comes from within. The common expression "He gets my goat" or "She makes me mad" is a fallacy. No one can do that to us without *our* permission. For Jesus, turning the other cheek was His strategy, for He did not allow the behavior of others to determine His response. Instead, He decided His course of action on the basis of His understanding of God's will.

This dramatic event marked the first of three Passover celebrations mentioned by John in this Gospel. (The other two are found in 6:4 and 13:1.) From this we would understand that Jesus's ministry was approximately three years.

Naturally Jesus's action in clearing the temple that day of the merchants and money changers created quite a commotion. And His timing was ideal—the city of Jerusalem and the temple were crowded with pilgrims who were there to observe the Passover. It is quite understandable that His action would be challenged. And afterwards the religious leaders asked Jesus for a sign of His authority for doing what He did (2:18). They failed to connect Jesus's actions, as the disciples did, with Psalm 69:9 (2:17) and demanded an explanation.

Jesus's response identified the center of worship as Himself, emphasizing the presence of God rather than ritual or ceremonies. John tells us that He spoke of His own body when He said, "Destroy this temple, and in three days I will raise it up" (2:19, 21, KJV). Then in verse 22 John further says that following the resurrection of Jesus, the disciples understood the Scripture and His words. But Jesus's opponents thought He was referring to Herod's temple, which had by then been under construction forty-six years. Instead of understanding His words as a sign of His authority, they thought He was playing games with them.

John tells us that "many people saw the signs he was performing and believed in his name" (2:23, NIV). This suggests John's awareness of other miracles Jesus performed during the Passover time and later, but he selected seven to illustrate the teaching he was led of the Spirit to share. It is interesting to note that John uses a distinctive Greek word for "miracle," one that really means "sign." He saw Jesus's miracles as far more than unusual and isolated actions. Instead, they were signs of what God was really like.

While it was true that "many believed in his name," John now tells us that Jesus was cautious and maintained a reserve because He knew they lacked a full faith commitment. The

Greek word for "believed" in verse 23, *pisteuein,* is also used in verse 24 to say that Jesus did not "entrust" (NIV) Himself to them. This helps us understand the same word that is also found in John 3:16, "that whosoever believeth in him"—whoever *commits* himself to Him—"should not perish, but have everlasting life" (KJV). We are called to a belief that commits, that identifies with Jesus. As Dietrich Bonhoeffer, a German martyr under Hitler, wrote in *The Cost of Discipleship:* "Only he who believes is obedient, and only he who is obedient believes."

The Word—as Regenerating Lord

The Christian life is a new beginning, a new relationship with God, a new Master, a new purpose, a new spirit. Jesus calls it a new birth. Being born from above means to have a new life generated within us through the Spirit of God. In contrast to what we do, in the practice of religion, the new birth is something that happens to us. We are to "be born again"; we don't "birth ourselves." The new life is the new relation with the Lord; we are reconciled to Him! And this is a corrective for our sinfulness.

We come now in our lesson to the fascinating story of Nicodemus's clandestine meeting and discussion with Jesus (3:1–21). John begins by telling us that Nicodemus instigated the discussion. This was amazing because Nicodemus was a Pharisee, an aristocrat, and a member of the Jewish Sanhedrin—he was one of seventy members of the "Supreme Court." And even though he came to Jesus in the dark of night, there was a ring of honesty in his opening comment:

"Rabbi, we know that you are a teacher come from God, for no one can do these signs that you do unless God is with him" (3:2, ESV). Despite his position, he came to talk with Jesus about the Kingdom of God.

Jesus opened His part of the conversation by giving Nicodemus a shock treatment: "Very truly I tell you, no one can see the kingdom of God unless they are born again" (3:3, NIV). Jesus was telling Nicodemus and us that knowledge about the Kingdom of God is not enough—he and we must experience a new birth of the Spirit. We are totally dependent on God's grace in being reconciled to Him.

Jesus told Nicodemus twice that he needed to be born from above, born of the Spirit (3:3, 5). The second statement was in response to Nicodemus's question as to how he could start over: "How can a man be born when he is old? can he enter the second time into his mother's womb?" (3:4, KJV). Jesus replied, "No one can enter the kingdom of God unless they are born of water and the Spirit" (NIV), meaning that each of us has had a "water birth," a physical birth, but He says we need second birth, a spiritual birth. Some commentators see Jesus's reference to being born of water as a reference to baptism, as with John the Baptist, and the spiritual birth as that baptism with the Spirit foretold by the Baptist. But at the very least, it presents the simple contrast between a physical and a spiritual birth in answer to Nicodemus's question in verse 4.

Jesus then went on to describe birth by the Spirit by saying it is like the movement of the wind. Just as we don't see the wind but we see what it does, so we don't see the Spirit but rather what He does in a person's life.

The words "the kingdom of God," or the rule of God, appear only here (3:3). However, this term is very prominent in Matthew, Mark, and Luke—especially in Matthew. But John rivets our attention on the Person of the King, under whose rule we are as members of His kingdom, His new fellowship of believers. Paul wrote, "The kingdom of God is not eating and drinking, but righteousness and peace and joy in the Holy Spirit" (Romans 14:17, NASB).

As the conversation with Nicodemus continued, Jesus was very attentive to his questions, and He moved on to interpret for him the nature of spiritual life, lifting an illustration from His knowledge of the Old Testament. Identifying Himself as the "Son of Man" in the Kingdom of Heaven (3:13), He foretold His suffering and death (3:14). When Moses lifted up the bronze serpent in the wilderness so that people looking at it in faith wouldn't die (Numbers 21:9), they were made aware that the God asking for this symbol of their death experience was their Healer. In this same way, Jesus said, He would be "lifted up" so that people would see, beyond Him (the human expression of God's grace), the very act and Person of God!

Now follows what we know as the golden text of the Bible, John 3:16. These few words express the Good News: "God so loved the world"—the *width* of His love—"that He gave His only Son"—the *length* to which His love has gone—"so that everyone who believes in Him"—the *depth* of His love—"will not perish, but have eternal life" (NASB)—the *height* of His love. Central in these words is the reference to Jesus as God's "only Son." The reference here is not only to the Incarnation of God in Jesus but also to God giving up His Son on the Cross

(Isaiah 53:12). Two important truths emerge in verse 17. First, we have the identification of Jesus as "Son" in relation to "the Father." Second, the word of grace is that God's purpose is not to judge but to save.

John now moves on to give us an interpretation of salvation (3:18–21). Here the focus is on our believing in the Christ as the Son of God. John uses the word "believe" ninety-eight times in his Gospel, highlighting the truth that we are saved by a faith relationship with Christ, our reconciliation with God.

Again John's words take us back to an opening statement in his Gospel, "In Him was life, and the life was the Light of mankind" (1:4, NASB). John combines light with its meaning of truth, for God's truth is the light of life. The contrast between the saved and the lost is between walking in the light and walking in darkness. We are children of light as we walk in the truth of Christ (3:21).

But there's a paradox here—too much light is no light at all. When we search for an object by flashlight on a dark night, we may succeed. But if we use a floodlight, we may become so dazzled and blinded that we cannot see. This is why God came to us in Jesus, revealing Himself in human form so that we could actually see Him. The dazzling and awesome glory of the eternal God would have been more than humankind could grasp. But here we see what God is like in the Person of Jesus Christ.

The Word—as the Son of God

The witness of John the Baptist is of special importance in the identification of Jesus as the long-promised Messiah. John burst upon the scene as a fiery, passionate prophet. His ministry strongly influenced that whole part of the country. People went in droves to hear him preach and baptize. Regarded by most of the people as a prophet, his words about Jesus were God's sovereign plan for the introduction of Jesus as the Christ, the Messiah. When the Baptizer was asked whether he himself was the Messiah, his answer was to point to Jesus as the Anointed One, the Messiah.

John the Baptist said:
- I am not the Christ; I'm sent to announce Him. (3:28)
- I am the attendant; He is the bridegroom. (3:29)
- I listen and rejoice; He speaks. (3:29)
- I am enlightened; He is the light of life. (1:6–9)
- I must decrease; He must increase. (3:30)

This part of our lesson (3:22–36) begins with a reference about Jesus's going from Jerusalem into the territory of Judea, probably in the neighborhood of Jordan but to the north of Jerusalem toward Samaria. Jesus and His disciples were now baptizing—apparently the actual performance of the rite was administered by the disciples only (4:2). The Jewish reporters informed John the Baptist of this, adding, "Everyone is going to him" (3:26, NIV). The depth of John's commitment is seen in his response, for having been the one to whom "Jerusalem . . . and all Judea and all the region around the Jordan" (Matthew 3:5, NASB) had flocked to hear and see, he now saw his followers turn to Jesus. But John insisted that was the way it should be; people are not to follow the preacher but the Christ, saying, "He must become greater; I must become less" (3:30, NIV).

In verse 29 John uses the illustration of a wedding party to communicate the goal of his ministry: "The friend who attends the bridegroom waits and listens for him, and is full of joy when he hears the bridegroom's voice. That joy is mine, and it is now complete" (NIV). In other words, John compares himself to the best man, not the groom. As in all biblical preaching, he pointed not to himself but to Jesus.

The final section in this chapter and of our Scripture lesson, verses 31–36, almost seems to be a continuation of what John the Baptist was saying in verses 27–30. However, they sound very much like the words of Jesus in the conclusion of His discussion with Nicodemus. This is seen if we compare 3:18 with 3:31, 35: "He who comes from above is above all. . . . The Father loves the Son and has given all things into his hand" (ESV). This suggests that the words may be those of the Gospel writer John, the one who is bringing together the Gospel account. This is a remarkable statement contrasting the earthly and the heavenly (3:31); expressing the testimony of knowing the truth of God (3:32–33); emphasizing the unlimited way in which the Spirit filled the life of Jesus (3:34); and presenting the relation of the Father and the Son (3:35). In fact, verse 35 is a parallel passage to the emphasis in Matthew 11:27 of the relationship of Father and Son.

This remarkable section concerning the deity of Christ emphasized (1) Jesus having come from heaven, (2) His speaking from a firsthand relationship with the Father, (3) His speaking "the words of God" (3:34), (4) His full identification with the Spirit; and (5) His full endowment with God's power as the extension of Father-Son love (3:31–35). As God's Son, Jesus always did the things that pleased the Father.

Believing in the Son and identifying with Him gives us everlasting life. This is the quality of life that we have in Christ—it never ends. In contrast, one who does not identify with Christ misses life (3:36b). God's wrath is His respect for our freedom to say no to Him without approving our no. God's wrath and God's love are two sides of the same coin—it is His sovereign control that will not violate our personalities while respecting our freedom for response. Our salvation is by His grace, His taking the initiative and moving to us. But God has moved, He has come to us in Christ; it is our move next.

Father, thank You for loving the world so much that You gave Your only begotten Son that we might have eternal life. AMEN.

A CLOSER LOOK AT THE GOSPEL OF JOHN

The Seven Miracles in John

"So the chief priests and the Pharisees gathered the council and said, 'What are we to do? For this man performs many signs'" (John 11:47, ESV). Many Bible teachers have called John 1:19 through chapter 12 "The Book of Signs." Like the seven "I am" statements, there are seven miracles, or signs, that point to Jesus as the Son of God. Each of these miracles demonstrated His divine authority and power through creative, transformative, restorative, providential, and life-giving acts.

The purpose of these signs is made clear: "that you may believe that Jesus is the Christ, the Son of God, and that by believing you may have life in his name" (John 20:31, ESV). Here are the seven signs, along with the references so that you can discover them for yourself.

1. Jesus turns the water into wine at the wedding at Cana. 2:1–11
2. Jesus heals the nobleman's son. 4:46–54

3. Jesus heals the man at the Pool of Bethesda. 5:1–16
4. Jesus feeds the 5,000. 6:1–14
5. Jesus walks on the Sea of Galilee. 6:15–21
6. Jesus heals the man born blind. 9:1–41
7. Jesus raises Lazarus from the dead. 11:1–44

The light shines in the darkness, and the darkness has not overcome it.

—John 1:5 (NIV)

Last night I walked the dog around the house. The moon hid behind a blanket of clouds, so it was darker than usual. Nights like this, I stay close to the porch, away from the shadows and things that might go bump or make the dog turn his head abruptly and stare at things I can't see—which freaks me out a little. It had been a long day filled with mishaps and work conference calls, and I wanted to move this short walk along so that I could go back inside and go to bed.

"Come on, Soda," I said. A slight warm breeze blew in from the south, and he pulled forward, heading into the darkness.

"OK, just a little ways," I said. For some reason, I let him lead. We walked down the hill, away from the house, where the shapes of trees were a hint darker than the sky. I was about to turn back when a burst of light caught my eye—and then another and then another.

Fireflies! The first ones of the season! They twinkled around us, like magic. I stood in awe, the brilliant flashes sparking a deep nostalgic joy, bringing a passion from the depths of my childhood up to the surface. Had we stayed by the house I would have missed this stunning display that lifted my spirit in a heartbeat.

—*Sabra Ciancanelli*

Notes

Notes

Notes

LESSON 2: JOHN 4–6

Christ the Reconciler— by Faith

✦―――――――――――――――✦

Dear God, as I read this lesson, awaken within me the measure of faith You've already given me. AMEN.

Someone has defined faith as "Forsaking All, I Trust Him!" Faith is our response to evidence; it is the action of our will when intellect and emotions are motivated by truth.

Actually, saving faith is no different intellectually and psychologically from any other expression of faith. For example, we exercise faith in our friendships, in our marriages—even in our business or professional lives. What makes *saving faith* different is that it is faith in the Savior.

In the mid-nineteenth century, the state of New York wanted to put a bridge across the Niagara River; authorities offered a prize of $10,000 (nearly $400,000 at the time of this writing) to the first person who could fly a kite across the gorge. In 1848 Homan Walsh succeeded. He used a lightweight string attached to a kite to pull a slightly heavier string across. He repeated this technique again and again, each time with a larger cord, until finally a strong cable was pulled across. This formed the basic support for the first footbridge, which had its start with the kite string.

In our first lesson from the Gospel of John we saw that salvation comes through believing in—having faith in—Jesus Christ. Now, in this lesson, John shows us the nature of faith. In this lesson, we'll see that faith as a response to evidence grows *with* the evidence. As with Homan Walsh's kite string, it may begin small, but it will grow.

Faith—Its Awakening

We are indebted to John for this marvelous yet shocking story of Jesus and the Samaritan woman at Sychar (4:1–26). It is a classic example of the awakening of faith.

The lesson opens with the news that controversy was brewing in Judea because of the success of Jesus's ministry (4:1–2). Rather than confront the growing rancor of the Pharisees, Jesus "left Judea and went away again to Galilee" (verse 3, NASB). But instead of taking the usual route—east to Jericho and across the Jordan River before turning north—Jesus headed directly through the hostile territory of Samaria.

Deep feelings of hatred and bitterness had separated Jewish people and Samaritans for over 700 years. When the Northern Kingdom of Israel was invaded and conquered in 722 BC, the Samaritans had integrated and intermarried with their foreign conquerors, which, from the Jewish perspective, made them unclean. For this reason Jewish travelers going north to Galilee nearly always took the eastern route up the Jordan gorge even though it took twice as long. But this time John tells us that Jesus "had to pass through Samaria" (4:4, ESV)—a statement of Jesus's sense of mission.

Next, we see Jesus arriving at a fork in the road near the Samaritan city of Sychar. It was noon and it was hot, and Jesus was tired and thirsty. While John emphasizes the deity of Jesus throughout his Gospel, he now pictures a very human Jesus, resting by a well (verse 6) while His disciples go into town to obtain food.

It was then that the woman of Sychar came out to Jacob's well to draw water. It may be that she came at noon to avoid the other women who had probably gotten their water earlier in the morning, for as we soon discover, it is likely that the women of the community shunned her because she had made a series of bad or ill-advised choices, as we see below.

Now we witness a marvelous lesson in personal evangelism as Jesus spoke to her and asked a favor. "Will you give me a drink?" (4:7, NIV). For Jesus, a Jewish teacher to even speak to her defied rabbinical law, and no good Jew would even touch a water vessel belonging to a Samaritan. Her amazement was real, but Jesus responded by talking to her about "living water." This not only caught her deepest interest, it opened the way for a discussion about the inner life. Ever sensitive to the needs of the people He met, and knowing her need was great, He asked her to "go, call your husband, and come here" (4:16, ESV).

She passed this test of honesty when she said, "I have no husband" (verse 17, ESV). It was then that Jesus exposed her sin. She had had five husbands, and the man she was currently living with wasn't her husband.

Upon realizing that Jesus was a prophet (4:19), she shifted the conversation to a theological issue. The Samaritans had long insisted that God was to be worshipped on their Mount

Gerizim ("on this mountain," verse 20, NIV) instead of in Jerusalem. Which was right?

Mount Gerizim had been the site of two significant altars in the Old Testament, one built by Abraham, the other by his grandson Jacob (Genesis 12:6–7 and Genesis 33:18–20, respectively). The Samaritans had worshipped there for centuries, and around 450 BC they had built a temple there. Jesus told the woman that "the hour is coming when neither on this mountain nor in Jerusalem will you worship the Father" (verse 21, ESV).

In response to the woman's question about the correct location for worship, Jesus told her that "salvation is from the Jews" (4:22, NASB), turning the focus to the arrival of the Messiah. He then declared that the New Covenant—God's new fellowship—had arrived! The woman apparently followed His train of thought clearly, for she immediately referred to her faith in the fact that the Messiah would come and would "explain everything to us" (4:25, NIV).

It is significant that Jesus's first declaration of Himself as the Messiah was to this Samaritan woman (4:26). She had been honest with Him, and whenever we come in honest faith to God, that faith is confirmed in His gracious acceptance. Her life was transformed, for she left her burden of sin for a new moral start. She left her religion based on a *place* for faith in a *Person,* and she left her bitter spirit for a new freedom and joy.

When Jesus told her and us that "God is a Spirit: and they that worship him must worship him in spirit and in truth" (4:24, KJV), He made it clear that God is Spirit-being in contrast to physical-being. Our worship is a reality of our spirits and not primarily of religious rites. Our worship "in Spirit and in truth" is elaborated in Matthew's account of the Sermon on the Mount, where Jesus moves us beyond act to attitude, beyond form to fellowship. And faith moves us to fellowship with God and our "neighbors" nearby and across the world.

Faith—Its Response

Many persons look for an answer to their hunger for God through pursuing selfish goals. But our hunger for God will never be satisfied with anything but Him. Archbishop, apologist, and writer Anselm of Canterbury (circa 1033–1109) prayed:

> *Help us to seek Thee in longing,*
> *And long for Thee in seeking;*
> *To find Thee in loving,*
> *And love Thee in finding.*

In these next verses in John (4:27–42), we see three expressions of the response of faith: (1) in the Samaritan woman; (2) in the disciples of Jesus; and (3) in the Samaritan people. In each case the disclosure of Jesus's Messianic role brought out a faith response.

The woman went back into the city of Sychar a changed person. She left her empty waterpot for a new life of inner fullness as she told the men of the city, "Come, see a man who told me everything I ever did. Could this be the Messiah?" (4:29, NIV). She left her burden of guilt for a new freedom of grace. And she left her poor self-image for a positive witness of faith. Now, as then, we cannot *really* be with Jesus and remain the same, and we cannot *really* be with Jesus without sharing, as this woman did, the Good News of new life in Him.

It certainly isn't surprising that when the disciples returned from the city, they were amazed to find Jesus sitting by the well in a public place and talking to the Samaritan woman (4:27). This just wasn't done! The rabbis taught that a man never talked to a woman on the street—not even his own wife. Once again, Jesus defied custom to meet human need—people, not rules, were important to Him.

Next, the disciples urged Jesus to eat the food they had brought back with them, but He declined, saying, "I have food to eat that you do not know about" (4:32, ESV). Once again, they failed to understand and wondered among themselves whether someone had brought Him something to eat while they were away (4:33). This, of course, wasn't the case. What He was trying to help them see was that His food—His source of strength—came from doing the will and work of His Father. Two other times in John's Gospel Jesus refers to the work His Father gave Him to do—5:36 and 17:4.

Now Jesus gave the disciples an insight into the mission of the Kingdom of God and what their response to faith should be (4:35–38). Drawing on an analogy of sowing and reaping, Jesus pointed out that beginning with John the Baptist, the seed of the gospel was being sown—now was a time of reaping: "Raise your eyes and observe the fields, that they are white for harvest" (4:35, NASB). They were being called into God's harvest field.

There is an important message for us today in these words of Jesus. There are more than 8 billion people in our world, and researchers suggest that somewhere between 1.6 billion and 3 billion of them have not yet heard the Good News of the Gospel of Jesus Christ. Then add to that members of our families and people in our neighborhoods and in our towns and cities who do not know Jesus as Savior and Lord. Indeed our fields today are ready for the harvest. To meet this challenge, it is important that we hear Jesus's emphasis on the team approach—as we work together, one sows and another reaps. By working this way our witness is complete and we avoid the individualism that measures success by our own achievements. In reality, our response of faith is to be faithful and leave the measure of success up to God.

In verses 39–42 we have the response of the Samaritan people to Jesus. First, John tells us that "many of the Samaritans of that city believed on him" because of the woman's testimony (4:39, KJV). Then the believing Samaritans went to see Jesus for themselves and were so impressed that they asked Him to stay with them for a time—and He did, for two days (4:40). And during those two days they came to really believe because of Jesus's own words (4:41–42, not just those of the woman at the well). As it was with them, so it is with us. We cannot exist on a borrowed faith; a true response of faith comes through personal commitment.

John closes this marvelous story with the acknowledgment of the new Samaritan Christians that Jesus was indeed the Christ—the Messiah—the Savior of the world. What a grand climax to Jesus's days in the village of Sychar! He had stopped as He traveled for a rest, for a drink, and for a noon meal at Jacob's well. But there He met deep human need and interrupted His travel north to meet that need. People in need were never an interruption to Jesus—and they should not be an interruption to us. Our busyness must never get in the way of God's business.

Faith—Its Integrity

Faith is response to evidence, and these next verses (4:43–54) focus on the integrity of the response. When we believe in the Person and victory of Christ, we glorify Him by acknowledging His actions and by acclaiming His authority.

When we pray in Jesus's name, we don't try to order God around as though He were our cosmic bellhop. Rather, through our prayers, we recognize His victory over sin and death by identifying with Him in that victory.

The scene shifts now from Samaria to Galilee, where John tells us that Jesus is enthusiastically received (4:45). In Cana, Jesus was confronted by a nobleman whose son was very ill. This concerned father had traveled the twenty or so miles from his home in Capernaum to find Jesus and ask for His help. "Sir, come down before my child dies" (4:49, NIV). Jesus's response was immediate: "Go; your son will live" (verse 50, ESV).

The nobleman believed Jesus and started the long trek back home. What a vivid contrast between the faith of this man, who was probably a Gentile, and the institutional Jewish religious leaders who were always challenging Jesus's acts and authority. The nobleman's simple obedience is a marvelous illustration of the integrity of faith. There is a lesson in this for us that is most important. We must not let the institutionalization of our religious experience keep us from being open to the creative acts of God in our lives.

Jesus's approach to the official's request was to first test the genuineness of his faith. "Unless you people see signs and wonders . . . you will never believe" (4:48, NIV). This is very similar to Jesus's dialogue with the Syrophoenician woman (Mark 7:27). But the father's response revealed the intensity of his pain and anxiety for his dying son and his full dependence upon Jesus. Seeing the father's reaction, Jesus responded with the good news that his son would live. When the nobleman heard this, he didn't demand proof of his son's healing, nor did he beg Jesus to lay His hands on his son. He simply believed and obeyed. This is the true character of faith, the ability to act on the promise!

On his return to Capernaum the official was met by his servants. This appears to have been the day following his request of Jesus, for the servants informed him that at the seventh hour, around 1:00 p.m., on the preceding day the fever had left his son. The father realized that the time the boy was cured coincided with the time at which Jesus had announced his healing. What a glad moment this was for the father and his entire family as they saw the evidence of faith in the well boy. The man's faith enabled him to respond to Jesus based on his understanding of Him as the life-giver. Here were living witnesses of John's earlier word, "In him was life; and the life was the light of men" (1:4, KJV).

John concludes this story by telling his readers and us that this was the second miracle-sign that "Jesus performed after coming from Judea to Galilee" (4:54, NIV). It is apparent from this statement that John did not intend to include in his select list of signs the miracles that Jesus performed in Judea (2:23). In the miracles that John did choose, we see illustrations of Christ's acts as creating and sustaining life.

Faith opens new dimensions of life beyond ourselves. As we have faith in one another, our personal lives are expanded. A lack of faith in others confines our lives to ourselves—to engage only in the limited circle of things that we can control.

In like fashion, faith in God opens our lives to all that God offers. A famous philosopher named C. E. M. Joad joined Bertrand Russell, H. G. Wells, and George Bernard Shaw in an attempt to discredit Christianity. But when he was in his seventies, Joad came to faith in Christ before the inescapable evidence and said, "The one whom I denied all my life I must now embrace!"

Faith is not a crutch, not simply a support for the weak. Rather, faith is the honest, humble awareness that there is more to life than what we can control and master; it is the privilege of relating our lives to the reality of Jesus.

Faith—Its Effect

We come now to the third sign (miracle) in John's Gospel as he tells us the story about a man who had been an invalid for 38 years (5:1–18). There was a possibility that after being incapacitated for so long, he had become accustomed to it. It is a very human tendency to accept ourselves as we are because in so doing we avoid the pain involved in change. Most of us can come up with a dozen and one excuses that justify our condition or position.

We meet this man and Jesus at the Pool of Bethesda in Jerusalem. Evidently, when Jesus saw him, He took a deep interest in him. There were doubtless many other disabled people clustered around the pool that day, but this long-disabled man became the object of Jesus's attention.

We next read that Jesus asked the man a rather curious question: "Do you want to be healed?" (John 5:6, ESV). In response, the man replied that there wasn't anyone to help him into the healing water. From this, Jesus knew that he was willing for change, and He extended His healing grace with the word of authority, "Get up! Pick up your mat and walk" (5:8, NIV). At once the man was cured. One word from the Master meets our need, for He is the Word (*Logos*) of God, and God's creative power is in this Word.

Earlier in our Scripture lesson we learned that there was intermittent moving of the water in the Pool of Bethesda. Some early biblical manuscripts include a sentence stating that people believed that an angel troubled the water and gave it healing powers (5:4), while others omit this reference. But the important message for us in this event is that Jesus didn't focus on the water but on the man's need. And in addressing that need, the man was healed. Jesus's own faith in the power and work of God was of primary importance. The man's faith to respond to Jesus's word effected a total change. He picked up his bed or mat and strode away (5:9), even though it was the Sabbath and the laws of Sabbath behavior strictly forbade this.

The carping Jewish leaders immediately condemned him for carrying his bed, which they interpreted as working on the Sabbath (5:10). He responded to their attack in verse 11 by telling them that the One who had healed him told him to "pick up your mat and walk" (NIV). And when they asked who had healed him, he didn't know (5:12–13). Jesus had left the man whole and had slipped away into the crowd, seeking no special attention. What a lesson in contrasts. Jesus had concentrated on the man's need for wholeness while the self-righteous religious leaders concentrated on his violation of the Law.

Later when Jesus met the healed man again, He told him to stop sinning lest he experience a worse thing (5:14). No doubt the relation of sin and brokenness is an intended implication of Jesus's statement, but in the largest sense Jesus called the man to a sense of responsibility.

Our difficulties are opportunities for us to experience the power of God. It is for us to decide what it is that we really want God to do for us. When Jesus asks if we want to be made whole, He confronts us with a conscious choice. It is for us to refuse or accept the compromise that surrenders to the status quo. The wholeness of God comes to those who seek Him. We will do well to pray with St. Augustine, "Enlarge Thou the mansion of my soul that Thou mayest enter in."

This part of the story closes as the healed man identifies his healer as Jesus and the Jewish religious leaders turn their anger on Him for healing on the Sabbath. And as John writes, they "were seeking all the more to kill Him" (5:18, NASB) after this incident. In response to their vicious attack, Jesus made this striking statement: "My Father is working until now, and I Myself am working" (verse 17, NASB). What a bold statement of faith! The Creator God continues to be at work in the world—creating and sustaining (Hebrews 1:3). This is our security—our confidence as we, too, are active in the work of God in our world today.

Faith—Its Assurance

The Good News of the gospel of Jesus is that we can become children of God. This is what it means to be saved—to be reconciled to God and to be in His family. And this assurance rests on the truth of Jesus. He is as good as His word! Again, we recall these words from the beginning of John's Gospel, "As many as received him, to them gave he the power to become the sons of God" (1:12, KJV).

We turn now in our lesson to Jesus's response to the Jewish religious leaders concerning His oneness with God the Father (5:19–47). How do we know that Jesus reconciles us to God? The answer is in His relationship with the Father. Jesus ordered His total life and ministry in the will of the Father. Here we see that

- the Father is the model for the Son (5:19);
- the Father loves the Son and works through Him (5:20);
- the Father gives life to the dead, so the Son gives life (5:21);
- the Father ties His honor to the Son (5:23).

The key verse on assurance in this passage is verse 24: "Very truly I tell you, whoever hears my word and believes him who sent me has eternal life and will not be judged but *has* crossed over from death to life" (NIV; italics added for emphasis). In hearing Jesus and believing in the Father we are given eternal life! Passing "from death to life" is a reference to the nature of salvation, for separated from God we have been spiritually dead (Ephesians 2:1), but in Christ we are made alive (Ephesians 2:5).

And this new life in Christ is both qualitative and quantitative. "For as the Father has life in himself, so he has granted the Son also to have life in himself" (5:26, NIV). This verse reminds us again of John's earlier word, "In him was life; and the life was the light of men" (1:4, KJV).

Jesus next moves on to give assurance that this life extends into the Resurrection (5:29)—that our lives are not bordered by either the cradle or the grave. In effect, this means that 50 billion years from now we will be living on with God! And this is true because of God's grace. It is also made clear in this verse that this resurrection unto *life* is for all who commit themselves to Jesus Christ as Savior and Lord. It is only those who refuse to believe, like the scribes and Pharisees of Jesus's time, who are condemned. As Dr. E. Stanley Jones, missionary to India a generation ago, wrote in *Victory in the Valleys of Life*, "If we will not take from the hand of grace, we will have to take from the hand of judgment."

We also see in these verses that the Father shows the Son everything He does (5:19), everything He thinks (5:22), and everything He wills (5:30–32). And the good news for us is that our relationship to the Son places us in direct relationship with the Father—He is *our* Father. This is an awesome, reassuring word for us.

Jesus then reminded His listeners that John the Baptist witnessed to the truth that He was the Christ but then added that the authority that the Father has given Him was the greater and final witness (5:36–38). And as further proof of His authority, He stated that "the very works that I do—testify about Me, that the Father has sent Me" (5:36, NASB). The "works" Jesus was speaking of here are the seven signs (miracles) that John selected to include in his Gospel. These are presented in chapters 2, 4, 5, 6a, 6b, 9, and 11—all are witnesses to His deity.

In the closing verses in this particular section (5:39–47) Jesus's listeners and we are reminded that it is possible to "search the scriptures"—to know the Scriptures—and still miss the Person of whom the Word of God bears witness. His listeners then—the Jewish religious leaders—prided themselves in the knowledge of their Scriptures, yet the love of God was not in them, and they were rejecting Him. Instead, they were more concerned about one another's approval than about God's approval. Some years later the Apostle Paul spoke to this when he wrote, "Study to shew thyself *approved unto God*" (2 Timothy 2:15, KJV; italics added for emphasis).

Finally, we understand from these verses that Jesus holds us accountable for what we know. In the case of Jesus's listeners who professed to know Moses's writings, they would be held accountable for everything that Moses taught, including recognition of the coming of the superior Prophet, the Messiah—Christ. In our case, it isn't religion that matters—Jesus must be taken into account, for only in Him can we actually be reconciled to the Father.

The words of assurance that Jesus gave us here are adequate for every problem and circumstance of life. All we need to do is take Him at His word.

Faith—Its Provision

Jesus is the Bread of Life (6:35). In Him and of Him we have our sustenance—everything we need for life. As God supplied manna in the wilderness after the Exodus to sustain the lives of the Israelites, so Jesus is our Bread from heaven, and only as we partake of Him can we truly *live* (6:1–40).

John now gives the fourth and fifth signs or miracles that are included in his Gospel: the feeding of the 5,000 and Jesus walking on the water (6:1–21). And they are not unrelated, for the feeding of the 5,000 is a sign that Jesus sustains life, and His walk on the Sea of Galilee is a sign that He secures life.

When God appeared to Moses in the desert in the burning bush, He gave His name as Yahweh, the One "I Am," self-determined Presence. In this Gospel John presents Jesus as using the same expression: "I am the bread of life"; "I am the light of the world"; "I am the good shepherd"; "I am the door"; "I am the resurrection and the life"; "I am the vine"; "I am the Son of God"; "I am the way, the truth, and the life." There are additional expressions that can be added to this list, such as Jesus's response to the Samaritan woman's comment about the Messiah, "I am He, the One speaking to you" (4:26, NASB), and His answer to Pilate's question as to whether He was a king, "You say that I am a king" (John 18:37, ESV). From all of this, we see that Jesus was clear about His mission, and we, too, need to be clear about our involvement in the Father's will.

These two signs occurred in the region of Galilee (6:1). First, John tells us about the crowds that thronged Jesus "because they were watching the signs which He was performing on those who were sick" (6:2, NASB), and then we see Him as He takes the twelve disciples up a mountain for a time of teaching. But it wasn't long before the crowd found them. They had probably walked several miles in their effort to catch up with Jesus, and when He saw them coming, His heart went out to them with compassion. Also, He had a plan (6:6). John sets this sign in relationship with the Passover (6:4), identifying what He knew was about to happen in the providing of food with the mercy of God in Israel's deliverance.

After Jesus had tested Philip (6:5–7), Andrew entered the scene with a boy and his lunch of five barley loaves and two small fish (6:8–13). Now Jesus acted in faith as He gave instructions for the crowd to be seated. He then took the boy's meager lunch, gave thanks for it, and it was distributed to the entire crowd. John tells us that when everyone had eaten their fill, the disciples gathered up twelve baskets of leftovers (verse 13). In this scene Jesus modeled by His faith in the Father how we are to believe in Him. Our little, given in faith to God, can become much as He multiplies it for His purposes.

John now moves us right along to the fourth sign (6:14–21). The well-fed crowd had been so impressed by Jesus's miracle-sign that they wanted to crown Him king, but Jesus quietly slipped away alone to an isolated place. When evening came, the disciples decided to return the few miles by ship to Capernaum without Jesus. As they were crossing, a strong wind swept across the Sea of Galilee, and while they were struggling against it, they saw "Jesus walking on the sea" toward them. John tells us, "They were frightened" (6:19, NIV), until Jesus said, "It is I; don't be afraid" (6:20, NIV).

In these two events—the feeding of the 5,000 and the meeting of Jesus with His disciples on the sea—we see signs of God's gracious acts in the sharing of His life and Himself with us now, even as He did with the crowds and the disciples then. And God's acts are never capricious but are always tied to the way He has worked throughout all history.

The next day, while talking with the crowds that had gathered again, Jesus built on these two miracle-signs by reminding the people of Moses. He explained, though, that it was not Moses but God through Moses who had provided their bread in the wilderness and who now sent the true Bread of Life (6:35). And if we believe in Him, we will never hunger or thirst again.

Augustine immortalized this whole thought when he wrote, "For Thy glory we were and are created, and our hearts are restless until they find their rest in Thee." In each of us there is a hunger for God that can never be satisfied with mere things.

The provision of grace is expressed in the familiar words of verse 37, "All that the Father gives me will come to me, and whoever comes to me I will never cast out" (ESV). That promise is for each of us, here and now. In faith we can come to Him with the certainty that He receives us, and it is in this faith that we can rest confidently.

The writer of the book of Hebrews put it this way: "There remains, then, a Sabbath-rest for the people of God; for anyone who enters God's rest also rests from their works, just as God did from his" (Hebrews 4:9–10, NIV). God stopped His work at the time of Creation, not because He was tired but because He was finished. We now can stop our striving and struggle and rest in the finished work of Christ. Dr. Thomas Dooley, missionary to Laos, said shortly before his death at the age of 35, "I believe the important thing is not how long we live, but what we do with the days allotted to us."

Faith—Its Discernment

There is a unique voluntarism about the Christian faith. Salvation is by grace—by God's initiative and provision. And our faith is a voluntary response to God's action. But God always takes the initiative. He moved first by coming to us in Christ. Now, as we face the truth of God in Jesus, we either respond in belief to identify with Him or in a disbelief that rejects Him.

In this closing part of our lesson (6:41–71), Jesus builds on all He has said and done up to this point, first by responding publicly (6:59) to the murmuring and questioning of the Jewish teachers and other leaders and then in private to the twelve disciples. It was clear then as it is now that not everyone is open to God's truth. When Jesus further interpreted the meaning of His redemptive mission as the "Bread of Life," many turned away (6:66). When that happened, Jesus then turned to the twelve disciples and asked, "You do not want to leave too, do you?" (6:67, NIV).

To that piercing question, Simon Peter answered in words reminiscent of his great confession at Caesarea Philippi (Matthew 16:16), "Lord, to whom shall we go? You have words of eternal life. And we have already believed and have come to know that You are the Holy One of God" (6:68–69, NASB). In these words we have the conclusion to which each of us is led in the discernment of faith: When we want to know God, we find Him in Jesus.

We see a vivid contrast in this part of our Scripture lesson between the Jewish leaders, who could not hear Jesus because of their prejudice, and the disciples who heard Him. And Jesus identifies and highlights this problem of prejudice—of lacking discernment of faith—by pointing out that even one of His own disciples was an antagonist and betrayer (6:70–71).

The character of their unbelief is shown in their arguments with the claims of Jesus. The prejudiced always have arguments for their position. The arguments of the Jewish religious leaders were (1) How can He claim to have come from heaven? We know His parents (6:42); (2) How can He give us His flesh to eat? (6:52); (3) This is a difficult teaching, who can accept this? (6:60). Disbelief can be changed to belief only by openness to the evidence, and they refused to be open.

Jesus then presented the basis for a discerning faith in His answers to those who were questioning Him. First He built on the truth expressed in the early verses of the Gospel, "The

law was given by Moses, but grace and truth came by Jesus Christ" (1:17, KJV), by saying,
1) Salvation by grace is seen in the primacy of God's call. (6:44)
2) No one can claim to know God and ignore His Son. (6:44)
3) No one has seen the Father but the Son, so a full knowledge of God comes only in Christ. (6:46)
4) Christ is the living Bread from heaven, the source of eternal life. (6:50)
5) The life Jesus spoke of was the life of spirit in contrast to the flesh—a life of fellowship with God. (6:63–64)

Also found in this particular Scripture lesson are two important theological truths. First, God's sovereign grace is expressed in 6:44 and 6:65. Second, the meaning of the Incarnation is expressed in 6:46, 51, 57, and 62. You may want to reread these Scriptures now in a favorite translation.

We began our lesson by defining faith: Forsaking All, *I* Trust Him. We close the lesson with this summary. Faith is deciding where to invest our lives. Faith discerns truth and acts upon it. Faith involves the total person—the mind in discernment, the emotions in devotion, and the will in decision. And like Peter, we are led to affirm, "Lord . . . you have words of eternal life" (6:68 NASB).

Lord God, You gave new life to the woman at the well, the nobleman's son, the crippled man at Bethesda. Thank You for giving new life to me! AMEN.

INSPIRATION FROM THE GOSPEL OF JOHN

Jesus said, "I am the living bread that came down from heaven. Whoever eats this bread will live forever. This bread is my flesh, which I will give for the life of the world."
—John 6:51 (NIV)

"Are you getting enough sunshine?" my doctor asked. He may have noticed my I-work-at-my-desk-all-day pallor.

"I work at my desk all day," I told him. "But I take vitamin D supplements."

He looked at my lab results. "Your calcium is on the low side of normal. Are you eating enough dark greens?"

"Not to worry, Doctor. I'll take a calcium supplement, or two."

This is how the appointment progressed in my mind as I prepared for my annual physical. I was compiling the list of medications and supplements, conscious that I was supplementing much of what the human body can normally get from a healthy diet and 10 minutes of fresh air a day.

How often do we try to do the same with our spiritual health? We depend on supplements—someone else's insights, Sunday's sermon, a brief nugget heard on the radio—as our entire spiritual intake for the week. We lean on supplements rather than a rich diet of daily Bible reading, prayer time, and reflection with Jesus.

Jesus no doubt carried on a perpetual internal conversation with His Father, but He still stole away by Himself for extended times of prayer. He said we should "abide" in Him (John 15:7, ESV), which seems more like a meal than a quick snack, doesn't it?

—*Cynthia Ruchti*

Notes

Notes

Notes

LESSON 3: JOHN 7–9

Christ the Reconciler— in Freedom

Dear God, open my heart and mind to the truths in this lesson. AMEN.

Receiving Jesus as Savior means freedom: "So if the Son sets you free, you will be free indeed" (8:36, NIV). There is freedom to be God's child, the freedom of the fellowship of the Spirit. Consequently, there is freedom *from* self-centeredness, freedom *from* sin, *to* worship. The quality of this freedom, though, results not in lawlessness but in personal choice. For example, if the doctor placed a handful of vitamin capsules on the table and said, "You are free to take all that you choose to take, but you should know that there are several that contain poison," you are not really free. On the other hand, if he said, "Help yourself, but avoid the red ones because there is poison in those," then you really have the freedom to choose properly. That's the way it is with law and grace: God's grace frees us to choose while at the same time holding us responsible.

Freedom—in Recognizing Truth

This part of our lesson (7:1–36) opens with John telling us that opposition to Jesus by the Jewish religious leaders had become so violent that He was now under the threat of death (7:1). For this reason He stayed close by the region of Galilee, where their influence was not so strong.

But we next read in verse 2 that the eight-day Festival of Tabernacles was at hand. This occurred around the middle of October, and every good Jew, if he could manage it at all, wanted to celebrate this festival in Jerusalem. Knowing this, Jesus's brothers, who at that time didn't really believe in Him, rather cynically urged Him to go to Jerusalem and give a public demonstration of His power. Till then, all His miracle-signs had occurred in Galilee.

It is significant to note at this point that while John's Gospel does not give us Jesus's temptation experiences in the wilderness, all three temptations are shown as present in His life. You recall that in the wilderness temptation event, Satan offered Jesus all the kingdoms of the world (Matthew 4:8; Luke 4:5–7), and in John 6:15 the people wanted to make Him king. Next, Satan invited Jesus to satisfy His hunger by turning the stones into bread (Matthew 4:3; Luke 4:3), and in John 6:30–31 the people asked for miraculous bread. And, finally, Satan in the wilderness experience took Jesus to the temple pinnacle and suggested that He jump off to show His power (Matthew 4:5–6; Luke 4:9–11), and here in John 7:3 His brothers urge Him to go to Jerusalem and demonstrate His power for all to see.

In response to His brothers' urging Jesus said, "My time is not yet come" (7:6, KJV). The word for "time" that Jesus used here is unique to this conversation—it actually means the proper time or "opportunity." He was telling them that for Him to leave at that moment would not be timely—for His purposes. Instead, as we shall see, it would be better for Him to go a little later so He could move into the scene quietly and select His own timing for action. Jesus stood free among His brothers and associates then and always to make decisions on the basis of His perception of the will of God.

John now gives us, almost parenthetically, the reactions of the crowd in Jerusalem as they looked for Him (7:11–13). Some said that He was a good man, but then, inconsistently, they failed to take His teachings seriously. Others argued that He was a deceiver and refused to hear His claims of being the Son of God. But whatever the perception, we read that fear of others prevented them from openly affirming that He was the Christ or even talking about Him (verse 13). The important lesson for us in this is that when confronted by Jesus, we cannot be neutral—we are either for Him or against Him.

John's reference to the hostility of the religious leaders in seeking to kill Jesus (7:1) occurs again in the dialogue we recounted in verses 19–24. They were amazed at His wisdom. However, Jesus had been well taught in the synagogue schools and was Spirit-guided in what He taught and did. In fact, verses 16 and 18 give us an important key: One whose teaching seeks a glory beyond himself has the authority that is commensurate with the one he glorifies, but one who seeks his own glory has *only* his own authority.

A basic principle of learning is that we learn by obedience to the truth. We educate not only the mind but the emotional, moral, and volitional (conscious choices and decisions we make based on our will) realms of life as well. Jesus said, "If anyone's will is to do God's will, he will know whether the teaching is from God or whether I am speaking on my own authority" (7:17, ESV). Obedience is a way of knowing. Just as is the case when learning a skill—like playing the piano or flying a plane—we learn by obedience in the exercises. So it is with discipleship: we learn by obedience, by decisions to follow Christ.

Verses 14–36 of John 7 may be called "the great controversy." First, Jesus's appeal to Moses was an indirect answer to their charge that He lacked formal education. In so doing He also demonstrated His skill in interpreting Moses's law. But His primary answer was that He spoke directly from God, not secondhandedly from Moses. He then argued from their own claims of accepting the authority of Moses to show them *from* "the law of Moses" the correctness of His gracious act of healing a man on the Sabbath (7:23). And in verse 24 Jesus concluded with the call to recognize judgment as a quality far superior to simple legalistic appearances.

Very cleverly and subtly Jesus was using His opponents' own interpretation of Moses's law to justify His actions of doing good on the Sabbath day. And He condemned them for their inconsistency in attacking Him. Again, it is easy for us today to be critical of those in that time who condemned Jesus's words and actions. But each generation of Christians, including ours, is beset by legalists who fanatically pursue their own particular letter of the law and lose the Spirit of Jesus Christ.

The focus now moves to the question of Messiahship, for Jesus's references to coming from God and His authority to interpret Moses's law are Messianic. As the people tried to dismiss Jesus by claiming to know His origin (7:27), He again affirmed His relation to the Father: "I know him because I am from him and he sent me" (7:29, NIV). In the face of the threat of arrest, John echoes Jesus's earlier words that "His hour had not yet come."

In the next paragraph (7:32–36), Jesus confronted the arresting officers sent by the chief priests and predicted in a parable His coming death and departure (7:33–34), leaving them perplexed. We cannot read this without being impressed with the boldness with which He taught in the temple and stood toe to toe with His opponents. From Jesus's example, we know that when we live daily in the presence of God, we need not fear any person or circumstance.

The need for open minds to recognize God's truth comes through clearly in this part of our lesson as we study the contrasts between the criticisms of Jesus by those opposed to Him and His answers and actions. He was accused of working in secret (7:4) and yet He taught openly (7:26). He was charged with leading people astray (7:12), but He responded by asserting that His teaching came from God (7:16–18). He was denounced for having never studied (7:15), but He said boldly that His teaching was not His own but God's (7:16). They accused Him of being demon-possessed (7:20), but throughout His teaching He honored the Father and stated so specifically later in this lesson (8:49). His origins were questioned (7:27), but He responded by declaring that He came from God (7:29).

Now, as in Jesus's day, only persons who are open to God and are free from prejudice are able to hear His truth.

Freedom—to Have Faith

The Festival of Tabernacles was the third of three great Jewish Festivals: Passover, Pentecost, and Tabernacles.

While observing the Festival of Tabernacles, the people left their houses and lived for the duration of the festival in booths constructed with branches from palm or myrtle, covered with a thatched roof, as reminders of their wilderness wanderings. It was a season of gladness—a time of celebration because the harvest had been gathered (Exodus 23:16). On the last day of the festival the people would march around the altar, and one of the priests would take a quart-sized golden pitcher to the pool of Siloam, fill it with water, and carry it to the temple, where it was poured on the altar as an offering to God. The people would then sing the Hallel (Psalms 113–118) to the accompaniment of a flute and recite the words of Isaiah, "With joy you will draw water from the wells of salvation" (12:3, ESV).

It was in this setting that Jesus stood and cried out, "If anyone thirsts, let him come to me and drink. Whoever believes in me, as the Scripture has said, 'Out of his heart will flow rivers of living water'" (7:37–38, ESV). Jesus is the true water of life.

This reminds us of Jesus's words to the Samaritan woman: "The water I give them will become in them a spring of water welling up to eternal life" (John 4:14, NIV). At the same time, Jesus may have been referring to Isaiah's words: "And the LORD will continually guide you, and satisfy your desire in scorched places, and give strength to your bones; and you will be like a watered garden, and like a spring of water whose waters do not fail" (Isaiah 58:11, NASB). It is very likely that

Jesus's listeners would have connected the Isaiah passage with His words. John interprets parenthetically for us, "Now this he said about the Spirit, whom those who believed in him were to receive, for as yet the Spirit had not been given, because Jesus was not yet glorified" (7:39, ESV).

Jesus is the One who gives the Holy Spirit—the Divine Presence—to those who believe in Him. We should note that John relates the gift of the Spirit to the glorification of Christ. The first real act of the risen Lord was to give the Holy Spirit to His disciples.

We now read that "there was a division among the people because of him" (7:43, KJV). Some said He was a prophet; others said He was the Christ, but His detractors argued that the Messiah would come from Bethlehem, not from Galilee (7:40–42). And still others wanted to get Him out of the way, to arrest Him (7:44). No one was neutral then, and we can't be neutral now—we either accept or reject Jesus. We have rejected Jesus in our time by our acceptance of a secular and materialistic way of life. Like the religious leaders of Jesus's day, we often reject Him when His teaching goes against what we want. But faith calls us to identify with Him, to follow Him.

The statement of the arresting officers when they came back to the chief priests empty-handed was a remarkable affirmation of Jesus: "No one ever spoke like this man!" (7:46, ESV). Jesus is the *Logos*, the Word of God, and His words are the authoritative declarations of God. No spokesman other than Jesus could say "I am the bread of life" (6:48, NIV) or "Whoever has seen me has seen the Father" (14:9, ESV).

Nicodemus, whose dawning faith led him to talk with Jesus (John 3:1–18), now spoke a word in His defense (7:51). But they taunted Nicodemus and asserted that no prophet ever came from Galilee (7:52). Yet they were wrong about that even as they were blinded to truth, for Jonah had come from Gath-hepher, just seven miles from Nazareth in Galilee (2 Kings 14:25).

Freedom to believe comes only as we are open to the truth of God that is above and beyond ourselves. To believe God we must look beyond what we tend to idolize as god.

Freedom—in Forgiving Grace

We come now in our lesson to a unique and moving story (8:1–11). In it we find a marvelous expression of Jesus's spirit of grace. The setting is the temple and it is early morning. Jesus is there, "and all the people came unto him; and he sat down, and taught them" (8:2, KJV). Once again the scribes and Pharisees enter the scene, bringing with them "a woman [who had] been caught in the very act of committing adultery" (8:4, NASB). A trap was being laid for Jesus by tricky scribes and Pharisees who wanted to catch Him in a bind between Roman law and Moses's law. For example, if Jesus didn't agree that this adulteress should be stoned, He would be violating Moses's law (Leviticus 20:10). On the other hand, if He sanctioned her execution, He would be usurping the power of Rome.

In response to their trick question, "Jesus bent down and started to write on the ground with his finger" (8:6, NIV).

According to tradition, the procedure of Roman criminal law was to write down the sentence on a tablet and read it. So in essence Jesus was saying, "If you are asking Me to usurp the functions of Rome, very well." John then says that "as they continued to ask him, he stood up and said to them, 'Let him who is without sin among you be the first to throw a stone at her'" (8:7, ESV).

What a master stroke on Jesus's part! By responding as He did, Jesus showed how mercy enriches justice. That is not to say that mercy excuses sin—it holds us responsible, for Jesus said to the woman after her accusers had left, "I do not condemn you, either. Go. From now on do not sin any longer" (8:11, NASB).

We have no way of knowing what happened to this woman after her dramatic confrontation with Jesus. But we do know that when we are open to His love and forgiveness, we are never the same again. To experience Jesus is to experience new life. And to really know Jesus should free us from a judgmental and condemning spirit toward others.

It is likely that this next scene in which Jesus continues His dialogue with the Pharisees took place in the temple treasury, located in what was known as the Court of the Women. This court was the setting for a massive display of candles that were lighted during a certain part of the celebration of the Festival of Tabernacles. It was in this brilliant, appropriate setting that Jesus declared boldly, "I am the light of the world. Whoever follows me will never walk in darkness, but will have the light of life" (8:12, NIV). By this reference Jesus continued His identification as the Messianic answer to the symbolism of their pageant: the living water and the light of life. You will recall that very early in John's Gospel, the Word—the *Logos*—is spoken of as "the light of men" (1:4, KJV).

The arguments in the verses following reveal a lot about Jesus as a Person. First, He stated that His witness was true because He had come from God (8:14). Second, His judgment was true because He spoke for the Father who sent Him (8:15–16). And third, His assurance was masterful, for He pointed out that in their law two witnesses were required for truth—He served as one witness, and His Father, invisible but present in the miracle-signs, served as the second (8:17–18). Then in response to the question, "Where is Your Father?" Jesus said that the Father was revealed in His very person: "If you knew Me, you would know My Father also" (8:19, NASB). Through their bigotry and spiritual blindness they failed to recognize their Messiah as coming from the Father.

John adds a note in verse 20 that gives us insight into Jesus's bravery at that moment. His enemies, the Sanhedrin, were looking for an opportunity to kill Him. Yet He was teaching boldly "in the treasury," practically next door to the chamber where the Sanhedrin met.

Jesus's boldness in declaring who He was within a few feet of His enemies' headquarters shows us that when we truly know God's purpose, there is no need to run from adversity.

Freedom—in Believing Him

We move now into a further exchange between Jesus and the Pharisees (8:21–30) that reaches its climax in verse 30. "As

He said these things, many came to believe in Him" (NASB). While other religions reach blindly in the darkness to find God, Christianity is the Word of God come to us, reaching down to us and laying hold of us. Christianity is not a religion *we* hold, but it is God laying hold of us, calling us by His grace.

Jesus said that He came from above. In contrast, while we are all of this world, He is not of this world (8:23). And the only way to know the Father, to know forgiveness of sin, is to know His grace in Christ. In His words, "Unless you believe that I am he you will die in your sins" (8:24, ESV). This is the first of three "if" statements in John 8. The second is found in verse 31 and refers to our obedience as disciples. And the third is in verse 36, which speaks to our freedom in Christ.

The references to His coming death reveal that Jesus understood the direction of His life (8:21, 28). He knew full well the cost involved in following the will of the Father.

When Jesus, referring to His death in verse 21, said that He would be leaving and His Jewish critics couldn't follow Him, they speculated cynically—hopefully—that He was talking about committing suicide. For the Jew this was a supreme sin that was punished with a special place in hell. So consumed were they in their derision of Jesus that they gave no attention to His warning about dying in their sin (8:21). The point Jesus was making was simply this: To reject Jesus Christ as Savior and Lord separates a person from God. And this applies equally to us today as it did to the Jewish leaders who were listening to Him in the temple.

Of special significance in this passage is the direct relation between Jesus and the Father. He *spoke* from the Father

(8:26). He *acted* on the authority of the Father (8:28). He *lived* in the presence of the Father (8:29a). And for His highest claim as to lifestyle, Jesus said, "I always do what pleases him" (8:29, NIV).

One of the unique theological aspects of these verses is Jesus's identification with God by the use of the phrase "I am"—"I am he" (8:24, 28, KJV). Jesus used the expression *ego eimi,* the "I am"—the very presence of God. This was reminiscent of Moses's meeting God at the burning bush in the wilderness when God identified Himself as "I Am."

As disciples of Christ, we come to His Word with our minds already made up to obey Him. We are called to live by His authority. And we are also called to live and act in ways that please Him. Our actions and attitudes are centered in Christ. We are saved in relation to Jesus, and we behave according to our relationship with Jesus. All of life is new in and through Him.

Freedom—in Belonging to God

The Christian life is one of discipleship. Jesus calls us to come follow Him, to identify totally with Him. This means that discipleship begins with faith in Christ, it progresses by obeying His Word, and it enjoys the freedom of His truth (8:31–32). In fact, it is in these verses that we find what could be called Jesus's great Declaration of Freedom: "And you will know the truth, and *the truth will set you free*" (8:32, ESV; italics added for emphasis).

Jesus's reference to freedom touched a tender spot in His hearers. They were proud of being children of Abraham and believed they were free in their heritage (8:33). But Jesus showed the deeper truth that all people are slaves to sin until they are set free in the freedom of Christ and belong to God (8:31–47).

Jesus's statement "If the Son sets you free, you will be free indeed" (8:36, NIV) is the key to understanding salvation. Jesus Christ releases us from the bondage and perversions of selfishness and frees us so that we can do the will of God. The freedom of the Son is freedom to be honest and consistent in our words and in our behavior.

The Jewish leaders had defended themselves and their actions by claiming to be Abraham's descendants. But Jesus contrasts their behavior with that of the great patriarch, saying that true children of Abraham would act in the faith of Abraham. After all, he had welcomed God's messengers when they visited him on the plains of Mamre (Genesis 18), while the majority of Jewish people in Jesus's day refused to receive Him.

In response to Jesus's perceptive comparison, his opponents now made the bold claim that they were children of God (8:41). Their claim was to a valid heredity: "We were not born of sexual immorality" (8:41, ESV). Some interpreters consider these words a derogatory allusion to Jesus's own birth, but not all Bible scholars hold this view. Instead, it may well have been a self-righteous defense. But Jesus countered their claim to having God as their Father by saying that if God was indeed their Father they would accept and love Him (8:42–43). And He then pointedly declared them to be children of their father the devil (8:44).

In telling the unbelieving Jews that the devil was their father, Jesus gave us a vivid description of the nature of the devil. The devil is a murderer and a liar, and those who do his works participate in his deeds. Also, he is the source of deceit and destructive acts. By contrast, the creative love of God enables us to support and serve others for their fulfillment.

Jesus had given them a clear word about His special relationship with God when He said, "I have come here from God. I have not come on my own; God sent me" (8:42, NIV). Now He contrasted this fact with Satan and his lies and put Himself on the line by asking, "Which one of you convicts me of sin?" (8:46, ESV). And then Jesus made the decisive statement that people either hear or don't hear based on whether or not they identify with God (8:47). To drive the point home, Jesus flatly asserted they were "not of God" (ESV), or, as the NIV states it, "you do not belong to God."

The question is not, first, Do we understand God? Rather, it is, Do we want God in our lives? If we want to know God and want to walk with Him, we will hear His Word.

Not everyone who observes the acts of God either understands or identifies with Him. Instead many people attempt to support God's word of grace with their own structures of religion. The famous architect Sir Christopher Wren designed the interior of Windsor Town Hall near London in 1689 with the ceiling supported only by the pillars in the outer walls. When the city fathers inspected the finished building, they decided that the ceiling would not stay up, so they ordered Wren to put in more pillars. Wren disagreed with their conclusion but knew he had to satisfy them, so he created an optical illusion by adding four pillars that didn't reach the ceiling.

While God does not deal in illusions, any pillars we try to add to His grace are useless.

Freedom—to Hear Jesus

The people whom Jesus had been talking to were enraged when He told them they did not belong to God. This was a stinging rebuke for people who took pride in their religious heritage. So they lashed out at Him by accusing Him of being a Samaritan, a half-breed—in other words, not a good Jew. And they capped that derisive insult by accusing Him of being demon-possessed (8:48). But Jesus responds calmly that He honors the Father while they dishonor Him with their unbelief.

Next Jesus made the amazing claim that "if anyone keeps my word, he will never see death" (8:51, ESV). From this we understand that one who knows God goes from life to life—from this life to the presence of God. Now Jesus's listeners were outraged even further, and they referred again to Abraham, who was dead, and the prophets who were also dead. Then they asked him, "Who do you think you are?" (8:53, NIV).

Again Jesus answered calmly but firmly that He honored and glorified the Father and the Father honored Him. The personal relationship with which Jesus referred to God is a revelation that we aren't to think of God as an idea or a universal principle or only as a source of being but as a personal, knowable God. Simply stated, Jesus speaks of knowing Him and keeping His word (8:55).

Jesus concluded this bit of dialogue with another of His great claims: He was the eternal Word. "Before Abraham was, I am" (8:58, KJV). This, again, was a deliberate identification with the God (Yahweh) who said to Moses, "I Am That I Am" (Exodus 3:14, KJV). There is only One who can say "I Am," and that One is God.

Jesus set His claims and revelation in the context of salvation history. All that God has done in the past has involved His *Logos*, His Word. And persons of faith have been those whose vision of God enabled them to see His person and His work. This accounts for the fact that Jesus was able to say that Abraham had actually seen the Messianic age to come (8:56). Their claim to be Abraham's seed (8:37) was now put to the ultimate test: Could they in the spirit of Abraham recognize the Messiah?

John's reference to the Jewish leaders taking up rocks to stone Jesus revealed their reaction to Him (8:59). They were closed to hearing Him as truth and so they judged Him a blasphemer.

The writer and Christian apologist C. S. Lewis once stated in *Mere Christianity*, either "this man was, and is, the Son of God: or else a madman or something worse. . . ." The more we understand of Jesus the more convinced we become that He was and is the one authentic person the world has ever seen. The question Jesus's opponents asked Him—"Who do you think you are?"—is still being asked today. And the answer is the same now as it was then.

The story of Signor Antonio of Minas, Brazil, was reported by the American Bible Society. Someone gave him a Bible. He vowed to burn it, and upon returning home he kindled a fire. But it would not burn. So, in order to make it burn better, he opened it. But the Bible never landed in the fire because his eyes picked out a few lines from Jesus's Sermon on the Mount. Arrested by its message, he read on further and became so engrossed that he read all night. As dawn broke, he stood up and declared, "I believe!" He heard Jesus and found the freedom to believe.

Freedom—to See!

In one sense, this part of our lesson (9:1–41) might be called "Freedom to be!" Here we have an encounter between Jesus and a man who had been born blind. Next John tells us that the disciples asked a penetrating question, "Master, who did sin, this man or his parents, that he was born blind?" (9:2, KJV).

The question assumes a direct relationship between sin and suffering, as was often taught. Jesus dismissed the relationship between sin and suffering by placing His emphasis on the presence and creative work of God in the human situation (9:3).

We learn an important truth from these words of Jesus: Ours is a precarious world in which accidents happen. But the Good News of the gospel is that we can invite the work of God into our difficulties and into the wrongs and weaknesses of our lives.

Jesus's emphasis here is on the "Light of life" that is come into the world, as He states boldly, "I am the light of the world" (9:5, KJV). And the function of light is to expel darkness.

As disciples of Christ we, too, are light in the world, punching holes in the darkness.

Then as a sign of this claim to be the light of the world, Jesus healed the blind man. Jesus's emphasis on the work of God (9:4) tells us that social concern and the proclamation of the Good News are companion expressions of grace. When we work to help others who are in need, we are manifesting the glory of God in our world today and are giving a positive expression of what God is like.

The sixth miracle-sign—the healing of the blind man—occurred on the Sabbath, the day of rest and release. But the religious leaders of the day, particularly the Pharisees, were so legalistic about the details of "rest," of no work, that they missed the personal wholeness the Sabbath was intended to provide. Even Jesus's act of making clay and anointing the man's eyes (9:6) was interpreted as "work," as violating their Sabbath laws. Because of this, the joy of the man's healing was lost in their censuring spirit of religious intolerance. It is said that someone once asked Friedrich Nietzsche, the German atheistic philosopher, why he was negative toward the Christian faith. His reply was a serious indictment against Christians of his time and ours. "I never saw the members of my father's church enjoying themselves." What a tragedy! And how contrary to the spirit of Jesus!

Jesus's emphasis on being the light of the world was evidently reason enough for John to include the entire story of the continuing dialogue between the Jewish leaders and the healed man (9:13–18) and his parents (9:19–25). The dialogue shows the growth of faith insight in the restored man and the darkness of unbelief in the members of the Sanhedrin. As they closed their minds to the truth, their only recourse was to try to confront truth with power. They excommunicated the man (9:34).

Significantly, the parents of the man had refused to speak up for the truth because they feared being excommunicated (9:22–23). But the man who had been healed, who had been touched by God, could not help but witness to the reality of his encounter with Jesus! This is the contrast between prejudice and conviction, the conflict between the raw power of force and the spiritual power of truth.

The actions of the Sanhedrin in response to the miracle were threefold. First, they examined the blind man to hear his story. Second, they examined the parents to confirm the story. And third, they re-examined and excommunicated the man who had been healed of his blindness.

In the examination of the man who had been blind, a division arose among his inquisitors because some of them recognized from what had happened that Jesus was a prophet of God (9:16). When the parents were examined, they copped out to save their necks. And in the examination of the healed man, we hear him begin to witness as a disciple of Jesus! His response to the Sanhedrin is classic: "One thing I do know, that though I was blind, now I see" (9:25, NASB). The old adage stands, "A man with an experience is never at the mercy of a man with an argument!"

A story is told about a poet and an artist looking at *Christ Healing the Blind,* a painting by the French master Nicolas Poussin that depicts the healing of a blind man in Jericho, another miracle related in the Gospels. The artist asked the poet what he thought was the most impressive thing in the painting. The poet complimented the expressions on the faces, but the artist shook his head and pointed to a discarded cane on the steps of a house. "There is the evidence of faith," he said.

The final movement in this remarkable story of healing occurred when Jesus looked for the man after he had been excommunicated and identified with him (9:35–38). The Jewish leaders had said that anyone who confessed Jesus as the Messiah would be excommunicated from the fellowship of Israel (9:22). Now Jesus turns the tables on them (9:39–41) by announcing the judgment implicit in His presence, for in the rejection of the truth of Jesus, the blindness of Jesus's adversaries remained.

Our freedom in Christ comes when we *see* Him as our Lord and Savior in every part of our lives—in the home, on the street, and in the marketplaces of our world.

Lord, thank You for being my teacher, my strength, my help, and the "lifter up of my head." Amen.

INSPIRATION FROM THE GOSPEL OF JOHN

"Let anyone who is thirsty come to me and drink. Whoever believes in me, as Scripture has said, rivers of living water will flow from within them."

—John 7:37–38 (NIV)

I love being near water. Whether I'm at the coast, a creek, or a lakeside, it settles me. But my favorite place is along the banks of the river running through my town in Oregon. The Willamette is wide, with beautiful old trees and countless birds calling it home.

As I watch this river, I sense Jesus's peace and power while the massive flow moves past with barely a ripple. Picking up stones to toss in, I feel my transformation as He smooths away my rough edges. When I spot fish struggling upstream, I understand the challenges they face. Jesus teaches me to push forward, to never give up.

Yesterday evening I walked the bank. The heat of the day was gone, replaced by a coolness hinting at autumn's glory. A gentle breeze carried the welcome scents of dust and falling leaves. As I rounded a bend, sunset lit the water's surface with a soft white glow, resembling molten silver. The image was emblazoned in my mind, depicting the way my soul is being refined.

  But the picture I hold close is of the living water that flows within me. Like a stone in that river, I'm following the course He's set for me through my obedience, rejoicing within the freedom of His boundaries. I trust His guidance around every bend, secure in the knowledge He knows the way. I'm willing and ready to guide others I meet along the curves of my life, leading them to Jesus and praying they never need thirst again.

—*Heidi Gaul*

Notes

Notes

Notes

LESSON 4: JOHN 10–12

Christ the Reconciler— in Truth

Gracious Father, sanctify me through Your truth: Your Word is truth. AMEN.

Truth is a unified whole, not just a collection of ideas. Paul, though, was very specific when he wrote to the Ephesians, "The truth is in Jesus" (Ephesians 4:21, ESV). And Jesus Himself said, "I am the way, the truth, and the life" (John 14:6, KJV).

Truth is personified in Jesus. He is the truth about God, the truth about genuine humanness. Jesus is the truth about divine grace . . . about salvation . . . about the Kingdom of God . . . about life and destiny. As John wrote in the opening verses of the Gospel, "The law was given by Moses, but grace and truth came by Jesus Christ" (1:17, KJV).

Truth—as the Good Shepherd

A shepherd tending a flock of sheep was a familiar sight in first-century Palestine. So Jesus now used this imagery to get across the idea that He is the Good Shepherd (10:11, 14) and His sheep follow Him because they know and recognize His voice (10:4–5). It was common practice in those days for shepherds to let their flocks intermingle. But with just a few words from their shepherd, the sheep would move apart from the others and follow the familiar voice.

The occasion for the parable (10:1–5) immediately follows the confrontation with the Pharisees over their spiritual blindness (9:40–41). Now as they listened to Jesus's words, they doubtless recalled the Old Testament references to God as the Shepherd of Israel (Psalm 80:1) and as Shepherd for His people (Psalm 23). Building on the imagery of the Psalmist, they identified themselves as being the sheep of His pasture (Psalms 95:7; 100:3; 79:13). The words of Isaiah (40:11) and Ezekiel (34:23) would also come to mind, identifying the Messiah as the Shepherd.

At the same time they would have remembered in those prophetic passages the condemnation of false shepherds. And so we find in Jesus's story here a denunciation of false shepherds while affirming His own unique role as the Good Shepherd.

There are three pictures of Jesus presented in these verses, quoted here from the King James Version: "I am the door" of the sheepfold (10:9); "I am the good shepherd" (10:11); and "I lay down my life" as the sacrificial lamb (10:17).

As the door to the sheepfold, He is the entry into the fellowship of the people of God, the way into salvation (10:9). It is only through Jesus that we are able to find God. He alone is the door; He is our security. After asserting His role, Jesus expressed the superlative character of His own mission:

"I came so that they would have life, and have it abundantly" (10:10, NASB). Life in Christ is the expanding life; it is life enriched by *all* of the resources found in fellowship with God! In contrast to the estimated 20,000 priests serving in the temple and some 7,000 Pharisees who served as teachers, Jesus stood alone as the doorway to life and to God.

The second picture is of Jesus as the Good Shepherd who (1) gives His life for the sheep—He puts us first (10:11, 15); (2) knows His sheep (10:14)—He identifies with us and cares for us; (3) extends His mission to those beyond the ethnic boundaries of Israel (10:16)—He cares for all; and (4) brings together all who hear His voice (10:16).

The voluntary nature of Jesus's coming sacrificial death is expressed in verses 17–18. Jesus knew that He would give His life in obedience to the Father's will—it would be no accident but rather an achievement. He would fulfill the nature of God's love in giving Himself to redeem humanity once and for all (John 3:16).

In this passage Jesus not only expressed the voluntary aspect of His coming death, but He also affirmed the victorious faith with which He anticipated death. He knew that at God's command He would be raised up again (10:18). And in Jesus Christ we share in that same faith as we face death, for Jesus promised to raise us up "at the last day" (6:54, NIV).

Once again John points to the division among the people because of Jesus (10:19–21). Some argued that He was insane and others said He was devil-possessed. But then there were those who said His words and actions were not those of a mad or demon-possessed man. Then and now—and throughout all intervening time—people are brought to a place of decision when confronted by Jesus Christ. We are either for Him or against Him. We either take God seriously or insult Him by indifference. And indifference is the ultimate insult—the opposite of love.

Truth—the Exposing of Unbelief

We are told now that the words and events in this part of our lesson (10:22–42) occurred during the Festival of Dedication. We know it as Hanukkah, and it was founded to commemorate the victory of Judas Maccabee over the Syrians and the rededication of the temple in 165 BC. It was winter, John tells us, the twenty-fifth of the Jewish month that parallels our month of December. The setting for this next bit of dialogue was "in the temple courts [as Jesus was] walking in Solomon's Colonnade" (verse 23, NIV).

Again a crowd gathered around Jesus and asked a penetrating question, "How long will you keep us in suspense? If you are the Messiah, tell us plainly" (10:24, NIV). "I did tell you, but you do not believe" (10:25, NIV), Jesus told them. He went on to point them to the works He had done in His Father's name as evidence of His claim. Jesus knew their question wasn't honest but was intended to entrap Him.

He knew they wouldn't understand Him because they weren't His "sheep." And then He went on to tell about (1) the character of His sheep—they follow Him (10:27); (2) the salvation of His sheep—they are given eternal life (10:28); and

(3) the security of His sheep (10:28b–29)—"no one is able to snatch them out of the Father's hand" (ESV).

In these electrifying words, Jesus was telling us that no power can overcome the Father; no one can come between us and Him. Paul expressed this in the marvelous words of Romans 8:38–39, "For I am convinced that neither death, nor life, nor angels, nor principalities, nor things present, nor things to come, nor powers, nor height, nor depth, nor any other created thing will be able to separate us from the love of God that is in Christ Jesus our Lord" (NASB). Only the human will, in the freedom of our own choice, can say no to God. Our security is that in saying yes to God, we are secure in Him. Jude wrote, "building yourselves up in your most holy faith and praying in the Holy Spirit, keep yourselves in the love of God" (verses 20–21, ESV).

The statement "I and the Father are one" (10:30, ESV) expressed the unity of will and purpose between Jesus and the Father. But this claim to oneness with God was heard by the Jewish leaders as blasphemy, and they took up stones to kill Him. Before they could act, though, Jesus took the initiative and asked, "I have shown you many good works from the Father. For which of these do you stone me?" (10:32, NIV). Their answer tells us that even though they had heard His claim, they refused to accept it. "'We are not stoning you for any good work,' they replied, 'but for blasphemy, because you, a mere man, claim to be God'" (10:33, NIV). They had asked Him to declare whether or not He was the Messiah. Jesus had responded by saying, "I and the Father are one"—but they refused to believe.

Jesus next revealed His wisdom and the shrewdness of His ability to argue with them (10:34–38). His appeal to their law enabled Him to declare His Messiahship—the Father had sent Him into the world (10:36), and He was right in claiming to be the Son of God (10:37–38). Jesus's words and His works were in agreement! Here is our model for all times as disciples of Christ—our words and our service of compassion confirm each other in the witness of the gospel.

John now tells us how intense their unbelief and hostility had become. Theirs was not a passive indifference but an active disbelief, a rejection, because He was an affront to their own position (10:39). John next tells us that Jesus escaped and traveled from Jerusalem "beyond the Jordan" (10:40, NASB). This movement of Jesus emphasizes just how critical and dangerous the situation was. It is possible that going to the region where John the Baptist had baptized Him and had designated Him as the "Lamb of God" was a deliberate choice—an identification with John's Messianic announcements.

We read in verses 40–41 that many of the people of this region believed on Jesus. The extent of their belief is expressed in their enthusiastic testimony: "Though John never performed a sign, all that John said about this man was true" (10:41, NIV).

Jesus knew, of course, what was ahead for Him. We've seen Him in this scene as He returned to the place where His ministry had started some three years before. His witness to His Father's message of salvation was clear and many believed. In this, we see our own mission for today. Ours is an insecure and threatening world, but we, too, are called to be faithful in our witness for Christ by words and actions in every part of our lives.

Truth—Discerning Divine Purpose

The truth about life is more than the natural mind can understand. Life is not bordered by the cradle and the grave. Billions of years from now we can be living on with God! This is resurrection hope, resurrection faith. We are not just persons with immortal souls but persons made in God's image, who are to be resurrected for life beyond time as we know it.

The story of the raising of Lazarus (11:1–16) gives us the seventh sign in the Gospel of John. Revealed in this event is the truth about life, about God's purpose of sharing the larger dimension of life with us. And the way in which Jesus postponed going to Bethany after hearing that His friend Lazarus was sick can only be understood by assuming that He was fully aware of the divine purpose in this.

John identifies Lazarus as the brother of Martha and Mary. Luke writes about the sisters but doesn't tell us about their brother (Luke 10:38–42). And here, in verse 2, we are told that Mary is the one who anointed Jesus's feet, but John drops this in as identification while that story is told later in 12:1–9.

Jesus apparently frequented this home in Bethany, a small hillside village just two miles or so from Jerusalem. In fact, it is quite likely that some of the time this was His "home away from home" when He was teaching and ministering in Jerusalem. Their friendship was a close one, so it was quite natural for Mary and Martha to send word to Jesus about their brother. "Lord, the one you love is sick" (11:3, NIV). And in verse 5 the Gospel writer expands on Jesus's relationship with this tightly knit family as he adds, "Now Jesus *loved* Martha, and her sister, and Lazarus" (KJV; italics added for emphasis).

Jesus's response, as He shared the news with His disciples, was to develop a progressive awareness of Lazarus's plight. First, He said, "This sickness will not end in death" (11:4, NIV). Next He said, "Our friend Lazarus has fallen asleep" (11:11, NIV), and finally He announced, "Lazarus is dead" (11:14, KJV). However, from the beginning Jesus affirmed that the illness of Lazarus was "for God's glory so that God's Son may be glorified through it" (11:4, NIV). And the glory of the Son of God *is His power over death*. It is this assurance that accounts for His announcements of His coming death without fear.

John now tells us that Jesus stayed on where He was for two more days before announcing, "Let us go to Judea again" (11:7, ESV). It was quite understandable that this word disturbed the disciples. They had left Judea for the country east of the Jordan River because of the threats on Jesus's life. Now He was going back into that hotbed of opposition! But He reminded His disciples that a day has 12 hours, a declaration that God's purpose will be fulfilled in the proper time. A day doesn't end before those purposes are completed, and our work is in the day when it is light, not in the night. Here Jesus's word picture moves to references to the light of the world, a metaphor that directs our minds to Christ Himself.

It is then that Jesus told His disciples, "Our friend Lazarus has fallen asleep; but I am going so that I may awaken him from sleep" (11:11, NASB). And when the disciples still didn't understand (11:12), He announced bluntly, "Lazarus died" (11:14, NASB).

God's intention was made clear in verse 15, where Jesus said that the purpose of the whole event was to enhance the disciples' faith. But they failed to understand this dimension of faith before the event. Faith is response to evidence, and that would come later at the tomb of Lazarus.

While the disciples lacked this dimension of faith, they had faith in Jesus, even if it meant death! Thomas summed up their feelings when he said, "Let us also go, that we may die with him" (11:16, KJV). Thomas's words tell us that the disciples were fully aware of the violent hostility the Jewish religious leaders had toward Jesus. They also remind us of Peter's words some days later, that he would die with Christ (Matthew 26:35), though when he reached that crucial moment in the courtyard of the high priest, he denied Jesus.

This certainly serves to illustrate the truth from Jeremiah, "The heart is deceitful above all things and beyond cure. Who can understand it?" (Jeremiah 17:9, NIV). The answer comes loud and clear through the Gospel story: God knows us and loves us anyway!

Truth—as Resurrection Power

There is a power greater than death: the power of life! And Jesus came to reconcile us with life. "I came that they may have and enjoy life, and have it in abundance [to the full, till it overflows]" (10:10, AMP). The miracle of raising Lazarus was a sign to everyone of the truth of Jesus's words, "I am the resurrection and the life. Whoever believes in me, though he die, yet shall he live" (11:25, ESV).

We turn our attention now to one of the most dramatic stories in the entire Gospel account (11:17–46). In studying these verses I want us to look at the four divisions in its development: (1) Jesus's conversation about the resurrection; (2) Jesus's deep emotion in the face of death; (3) Jesus's call that awakes the dead; (4) Jesus total rejection by the religious leaders.

In the other Gospels there are accounts of Jesus raising people from the dead: Jairus's daughter (Matthew 9:18–26) and the widow's son at Nain (Luke 7:11–16). In both of these cases, life was restored soon after death, and some people might dismiss them as resuscitation. But Lazarus had been dead for *four days*! Here, without question, was a full witness to resurrection power.

Jesus's conversation with Martha (11:20–28) is a most significant treatment of resurrection. There was no uniform or common belief among the Jewish parties about life after physical death. On one hand, the Sadducees did not believe in the resurrection. But the Pharisees held a strong belief in a resurrection from the dead. Undoubtedly, these conflicting beliefs had been discussed in Lazarus's home.

But let's look now at the conversation between Jesus and Martha. When He arrived on the outskirts of Bethany, she greeted Him by saying, "Lord, if you had been here, my brother would not have died" (11:21, ESV). It sounds very much as if she was chiding Jesus for His delay in getting there.

But then her faith in the Lord took over and she added, "But even now I know that whatever you ask from God, God will give you" (11:22, ESV).

Now notice Jesus's response: "Your brother will rise again" (11:23, NIV). Martha then affirmed her belief in the resurrection—life beyond the grave (11:24). She had come to the heart of faith that could affirm the Father's promise, "I will raise him up at the last day" (6:40, KJV). The highwater mark of Old Testament hope had become clear for her; she could then say with Job, "And after my skin has been destroyed, yet in my flesh I will see God; I myself will see him with my own eyes—I, and not another" (Job 19:26–27, NIV). Now came some of Jesus's grandest words, "*I am the resurrection and the life*; the one who believes in Me *will live*, even if he dies, and everyone who lives and believes in Me *will never die*" (11:25–26, NASB; italics added for emphasis).

When Martha heard those words, she made her soul-changing confession that Jesus was in truth the Messiah—the Son of God (11:27). Undoubtedly, there was more to the conversation than John wrote down, for Martha left Jesus, hurried home, and told her sister, Mary, "The Teacher is here and is calling for you" (11:28, NASB).

What a marvelous reminder in any time of difficulty—Jesus is here with us, just as He was with Martha and Mary in their time of sorrow. To know God's compassion, His caring, is enough to transform every difficulty into a possibility. And to have the added personal word that He "is calling for you" means that Jesus was particularly concerned about Mary—even as He is for you and me. What was Mary's response to this good news? "She arose quickly, and came unto him" (11:29, KJV). That says it all!

In the next scene we see Jesus confronted by the weeping Mary and surrounded by the attending mourners. The depth of His grief comes through in John's vivid words, "He was deeply moved in his spirit and greatly troubled" (11:33, ESV). Jesus had lost a close friend, but more important, we catch a glimpse of how deeply He felt about death. God is not an unfeeling, distant being but a God who shares and participates in the anguish of His people. The two short words of the shortest verse in the Bible express the depth of God's caring: "Jesus wept" (11:35, KJV). And "deeply moved" within Himself, fully aware of the weight of His conflict with death, Jesus made His way to the cave that was Lazarus's grave (11:38).

After telling the mourners to remove the stone from the mouth of the cave and responding to Martha's concern about the condition of her brother's body, Jesus prayed an intimate prayer to His Heavenly Father. Upon the conclusion of that short but confident prayer, Jesus shouted, "Lazarus, come forth" (11:43, KJV). And then the crowd saw "the glory of God" as Lazarus shuffled out of the cave.

Jesus knew the dead could hear His voice and would respond. As the Victor over death, Jesus reached into the region of the departed and brought Lazarus back and reunited him with his sisters and friends. The reconstituting of a wasted body was a secondary miracle in relation to the primary one—Lazarus was back!

As we picture these events, we can't help but wonder what Jesus felt as He looked at His old friend. But even in the middle of this awesome scene, Jesus had the presence of mind to say, "Loose him, and let him go" (11:44, KJV).

John next gives us the reaction of the crowd: "Many . . . believed in him" (11:45, ESV). But others, filled with self-righteous bigotry, turned their backs on what Jesus had done and carried a tale to the conniving Pharisees (11:45–46).

We have in this part of our lesson a ring of truth that we are meant to hear. God is at work in our world even today as we rush pell-mell through the twenty-first century. Our mission is to be open—to *listen* and to *see*. If we shut out avenues of truth and people who worship God and live for Him in ways that differ from ours, we may well miss the awesome and majestic glory of God and the difference it makes in the lives of people who are pressing toward that glory.

Truth—Confronting the Powers

Earthly power tends toward idolatry. It becomes an end in itself, an ultimate. As Sir John Dalberg-Acton (1834–1902) once said, "Power tends to corrupt, and absolute power corrupts absolutely." Power of position has a problem with the power of truth. Justice calls for equality of opportunity for all persons, but the structures of power build a pyramid and trap the people at the lower levels as servants to those at the upper levels. But such power structures are threatened when those at the lower levels are treated with equal privilege as the leaders.

In this part of our lesson now the Sanhedrin, a Jewish governing body made up of both Pharisees and Sadducees, is assembled to plan what to do about Jesus (11:47–53). His type of power, the Messianic power of redemptive love, of reconciling grace, challenged the uses of power for the dominance of one group of people by another. The threat to the Sanhedrin was seen by them as a threat to Rome, the power structure to which they answered. After all, if Jesus in any way created a public uprising or disorder, their position would be threatened. They had to get rid of Him and His reconciling power, which was in sharp opposition to their self-interests.

In response to the Sanhedrin debate about Jesus, the words of Caiaphas were bold and crude, matching the pattern of the arrogant Sadducees: "You know nothing at all!" (11:49, NIV). In so many words he was saying, "If you had any sense, you would know . . . ." Continuing in verse 50, the high priest went on to say, "It is better for you that one man die for the people than that the whole nation perish." It is ironic that Caiaphas, in making this speech, was actually foretelling Jesus's vicarious death without realizing it (11:51). John interprets the words as a prophecy of Jesus's redemptive work in His death, to "gather together in one the children of God that were scattered abroad" (11:52, KJV). In other words, Jesus, in His death, would demonstrate the reconciling truth that draws everyone from the sin of self-structures to the fellowship of a gracious, self-giving God.

Jesus was not reckless, so because of the violent hostility of His enemies, He withdrew to the hills north of Jerusalem to Ephraim in the region of Bethel (11:54–57). But in the

Jewish community, Jesus was now a fugitive with a price on His head. The Sanhedrin ordered the people to report on Jesus, to tell them where He was located. The sinister conspiracy against Jesus was gaining momentum, and John now tells us that the people, who were gathering to purify themselves in the temple court in preparation for the Passover, were discussing among themselves whether Jesus would put in an appearance at the feast.

Truth—in Messianic Announcement

John's selection of the three unique scenes of this section of our study (12:1–36) presents three aspects of Jesus's reconciling work: (1) the preparation for His suffering and death; (2) the announcement of His role as King of kings; and (3) the universal nature of His redemptive mission.

In scene 1 (12:1–9) Jesus had come out of seclusion and was in Bethany at the home of Lazarus. Once again Jesus was among friends who loved Him, and they were enjoying dinner together on the Saturday evening before Palm Sunday as we know it. Martha, true to form, was serving dinner. Lazarus sat at the table with Jesus, and an assortment of curious people filled the courtyard of this wealthy home to get a look at the resurrected Lazarus, as well as at Jesus (12:9).

But the main actor in this drama was Mary, the sister, who brought a pound of nard, an oriental ointment that had cost "three hundred denarii" (12:5, ESV)—a whole year's wages for a day laborer—and poured it on Jesus's feet. In an act of humble devotion she loosed her hair and wiped His feet. The fragrance filled the house, and everyone became aware of her gesture of love. Love has a way of enriching the whole community. Love gives its all, for Jesus's love was to give all—Himself.

This scene also introduces Judas Iscariot as a negative voice (12:4–5). His crass materialism blinded him to Mary's expression of love. He counted the cost, and we learn of the extent of Mary's extravagance through his ill-mannered criticism. Judas, like most critics, attempted to cover his real motive with a good face, for he asked, "Why was this ointment not sold . . . and given to the poor?" (12:5, KJV). But John explains that he didn't ask this out of concern for the poor but because he was a thief (12:6), and as treasurer for the group, he probably helped himself to the funds. This interpretation by the writer was possible because of the temporal distance from the event in which the Gospel was written. The disciples were unaware of Judas's deceit until well after the Bethany event.

Jesus responded to Judas's criticism of Mary by saying that the ministry to the poor could be fulfilled at any time, but to prepare for His death could only be done now (12:8). There is always the proper time to share love, and when the opportunity passes, it rarely comes again to any of us in the same way.

The second scene is the triumphal entry into Jerusalem (12:10–19). John injects a reference in this account to the Sanhedrin wanting to kill Lazarus to destroy the living evidence to Jesus's miracle—further proof of their violent hostility toward Jesus. The primary emphasis in this scene, though, is on the courage of Jesus as He rode publicly through the crowds of Passover pilgrims into Jerusalem in the face of His enemies. That He came on the back of a lowly donkey rather than on a charging white horse speaks of the peaceful nature of the Messiah. Jesus did not ride into the city as a conquering king but as the Prince of Peace. This must have been a fearsome and awesome moment for Jesus's close followers. While the crowds along the road that day seemed to welcome Him, the disciples knew of the death threats that had been made against Him. But John now tells us that they didn't understand what all of this meant until after Jesus's death, resurrection, and ascension (12:16). Only then did they connect these events with the Old Testament prophecies, including Zechariah (9:9).

At the same time, Jesus's enemies among the Jewish religious leaders were dumbfounded, frustrated, and furious. To them it seemed He had flaunted His presence when He openly rode into Jerusalem on that first Palm Sunday. But they didn't dare take Him then because of the crowd's enthusiasm. "Look how the whole world has gone after him!" (12:19, NIV).

The third scene, given to us only in John's Gospel, is a moving occasion that signals the interest in Jesus by the Gentile world in contrast to Jewish unbelief (12:20–36). Some Greeks, possibly involved in their customary search for truth, were in Jerusalem. They may well have been looking into the worship of Jehovah. Certainly, their inquiry of Philip gives us a striking focus on worship: "Sir, we wish to see Jesus" (12:21, ESV). Perhaps they had been in the crowd when Jesus cleansed the Gentile Court of the temple, and now they wanted to meet Him personally. In response to their request, Philip took them to his brother Andrew, and once again we focus our attention on Andrew as the one who took people to Jesus (12:22).

Without doubt, Andrew is a prime model for us today as we seek to fulfill our witness.

Jesus took this opportunity to declare some important truth. In verse 23 He announced, "The hour has come for the Son of Man to be glorified" (NIV). This was likely an electrifying statement to religious leaders who were listening because of their traditional understanding of what it meant for the Son of Man to be glorified. They would have interpreted this as the long-looked-for moment when the conquering Messiah would move across the world and subdue all their enemies. But when Jesus used the word "glorified," He was referring to His coming death on the Cross.

Then Jesus's words in verses 25–26 responded directly to the Greek philosophy of self-esteem that was so prevalent in the world at that time—and still is today. The Jesus way of life is that of the Suffering Servant: The seed falls into the ground and dies before it can give new life. "The one who loves his life loses it, and the one who hates his life in this world will keep it to eternal life" (12:25, NASB). This contrast between powers and service, between self-fulfillment and discipleship of Christ, continues to be just as much the point of decision in faith today as it was when John's Gospel was written.

While John in his Gospel does not include the picture of Jesus's agony in the Garden of Gethsemane, we do catch something of that struggle in the prayerful expression of Jesus found in verses 27–28. Here His servant role is responded to by a confirming voice from heaven. Jesus interpreted this as a sign of the purpose of God and of the judgment of God exposing and completely defeating the devil—"the prince of this world" (12:31, KJV). And then, right in the middle of this victory passage, Jesus referred to His coming death, "And I, when I am lifted up from the earth, will draw all people to myself" (12:32, ESV).

From our vantage point in history, we can look back and testify to the fact that truer words were never spoken. Jesus's words and message have touched every generation across the world since His "glorification." And this will continue to the end of time.

Jesus's final words in this section call for His listeners to walk in the light—in the truth of God. And with that, He withdrew from them and hid, leaving them to ponder the implication of the truth they had heard.

Truth—and the Blindness of Unbelief

In this closing movement of our lesson (12:37–50) we confront the truth that unbelief is not passive; it is an active disbelief. It is a choice to reject the truth. In the face of the many miracles Jesus wrought, the unbelieving people continued to reject Him (12:37). John then quotes the prophet Isaiah to show how their unbelief did not alter God's purpose of redemption. The acts of reconciliation by a gracious God are genuine acts, and when the people of Israel satisfied themselves with religion rather than with God, the divine revelation was given in spite of their unbelief. Since the people didn't want God, He in turn kept them from fully understanding, lest their response of converting be a response to truths without being a desire for the Truth!

There is a significant contrast between Isaiah with his vision of God's glory (12:41) and the chief rulers who believed in God's Son but who were too concerned about their religious positions to confess Him (12:42–43). It was true then, and it is true now, that when people love the praise of men more than the praise of God, they continue in unbelief. Earlier, Jesus had spoken to this fatal flaw when He said, "How can you believe, when you receive glory from one another and do not seek the glory that comes from the only God?" (5:44, ESV).

Jesus now concluded the temple teaching with some pointed declarations, as translated in the New American Standard Bible:

1) "The one who sees Me sees Him who sent Me." (12:45)
2) "I have come as Light into the world, so that no one who believes in Me will remain in darkness." (12:46)
3) "I did not come to judge the world, but to save the world." (12:47)
4) "The word which I spoke. That will judge him on the last day." (12:48)
5) "For I did not speak on My own, but the Father Himself who sent [gave] Me has given Me a commandment as to what to say and what to speak." (12:49)
6) "I know that His commandment is eternal life." (12:50)
7) "The things I speak, I speak just as the Father has told Me." (12:50)

The seven great declarations give us a concise statement of the Good News of God's reconciling grace for all people of all time. The gospel is the truth of God's action to reestablish a right relationship between sinful people and Himself.

Loving Lord, thank You for the privilege of being one of Your sheep and of being able to distinguish Your voice over the clamor of my days. A<small>MEN</small>.

INSPIRATION FROM THE GOSPEL OF JOHN

Then Jesus said, "Did I not tell you that if you believe, you will see the glory of God?"

—John 11:40 (NIV)

"You have cancer." My fingers tightened on the receiver as the receptionist spoke. Details spilled out like water from a dropped glass—the type, stage, and post-surgery possibilities. Depending on the tumor's size, I could lose a breast and require reconstructive surgery. I concentrated on keeping my voice even and held back tears, at least until I'd hung up. The only words that came to mind were "Why me, Jesus? Why now?"

The weeks following that diagnosis were lost in a fog. Time alternately flew and dragged, as I waited to endure my procedure. My operation was a success, but ensuing radiation treatments left me confused, as if I were watching someone else's life through a pair of binoculars. I clung to Jesus, His abiding love my private sanctuary. My faith strengthened even as my body weakened.

Over several months, my self-confidence grew and my health returned. All five senses came alive, awakening a hunger for new experiences. Bit by bit, clarity of thought reappeared and, with it, a new wisdom and gratefulness. Little things no longer bothered me. I became more aware of the blessings surrounding me. I learned that, like Lazarus, I wasn't alone. Friends, family, and Jesus had cried and prayed for me. And during that battle, I realized the true value of a life I'd taken for granted. I didn't have to die to rise again. Our Lord restored me, body and soul. At last I have the answer to the question "Why?"

—*Heidi Gaul*

Notes

Notes

Notes

LESSON 5: JOHN 13–15

Christ the Reconciler— in Fellowship

O God, use this lesson to teach me the utmost importance of having fellowship with You. AMEN.

Reconciliation with God brings us into His family. As His children through faith in Christ, we can look up and say, "Abba, Father." We belong, we fit at the throne, we have been given the "power to become the sons of God" (1:12, KJV). In Jesus we discover how children of God conduct themselves. And in belonging to God's family we must relate in love to the rest of His family.

The other Gospels tell of the Passover meal, and of the institution of the Lord's Supper. John shares the scene of foot washing and goes on to relate the extensive teaching that Jesus gave the disciples during and at the close of the meal.

Fellowship—through Loving Service

The washing of the disciples' feet is one of the most remarkable symbols of Jesus's humility and service (13:1–17). Take a moment now to read those seven verses in your preferred translation of the Bible.

First, John tells us of Jesus's full understanding of His relationship to His coming death, to His disciples, and to His Heavenly Father (13:1–3). The statement "that he was come from God, and went to God" supplies the contrast for the humble act of foot washing that follows. These words remind us of the great Incarnation passage in Philippians 2:5–11 where Paul affirms that Jesus was in very nature God . . . He became in very nature man . . . He humbled Himself and became obedient unto death!

It was the custom in Jesus's time that as guests arrived at a house, a servant would supply water and wash their feet. But there had been no servant present on this occasion, and while John doesn't tell us, Luke described the bickering that was going on among the disciples as to which one would be the greatest in the Kingdom (Luke 22:24). This certainly hadn't produced a climate wherein any of the disciples would stoop to perform the cleansing task, so this nicety had just been bypassed and they had gone on with the supper.

Jesus, of course, was very conscious of their concern over status and took this as the occasion to model for them the role of serving. John says, "Jesus . . . rose from supper . . ." (13:3–4, ESV). In the Passover service there were four cups of wine that were drunk, interspersed with four promises of God. The first was with the promise "I will bring you out." Following these words, the food was brought in and the meal was presented. Then this question was asked: "Why is this night different from any other night?" The answer, of course, related the night to their Exodus from Egypt, and this was followed by singing the short Hallel (Psalms 113–115).

The second cup was drunk with the promise "I will rid you of your bondage." Unleavened bread was then dipped in the dish with bitter herbs, and the head of the family prayed, "Blessed art Thou, O Lord God, King of the universe, who bringeth forth bread to eat . . ." The main course was then eaten—all of a roasted lamb was consumed.

The third cup was then drunk and comments were made on the expectation of the Messiah. It was at this stage in the meal that Jesus introduced "the Lord's Supper," with the symbols of His death. At the Passover meal there was normally a period of fellowship before the fourth cup was drunk. Evidently, it was at this time that Jesus got up, laid aside His outer robe, and took a towel and basin and began to wash the disciples' feet.

Later the fourth and final cup would have been shared, with the traditional words, "I will be your God and you will be my people." Then the meal closed with the singing of the last Hallel (Psalms 116–123).

Throughout the story, John shows us the full extent of Jesus's love: "Having loved his own who were in the world, he loved them to the end" (13:1, NIV). Jesus's love is seen here as He stoops to serve His disciples, as He keeps the way open for Judas to repent, as He teaches the disciples that true greatness is found in serving others (13:16; see also Luke 22:27).

As we follow Jesus in the everyday routines of our lives, we discover the greatness of serving Him in our service for others. It is the little things that enhance another person's well-being; it is in the humble acts of self-giving for the enrichment of other people that we are able to express and live out the spirit of Jesus. Jesus reminded us of this eternal truth when He said, "To the extent that you did it for one of the least of these brothers or sisters of Mine, you did it for Me" (Matthew 25:40, NASB).

Fellowship—in the Lord's Supper

Fellowship is not blind; it is discerning. Our togetherness in love and acceptance is not a cover-up. We don't ignore or approve each other's limitations and shortcomings, but we refuse to allow them to disturb or impair our fellowship. Jesus was aware of the selfish ambition of Judas that led to his infamous act of betrayal. Jesus was aware of Peter's impulsive self-assertion that wasn't always backed up with inner strength—a weakness that led to Peter's denial of the Lord. And yet Jesus communicated to each one of His disciples His constant love. This truth is beautifully illustrated in this next scene in our lesson (13:18–38).

Apparently Judas had been present when Jesus washed the disciples' feet. We can imagine that when Jesus came to Judas that evening, He had been especially tender, as if to say, "Judas, I haven't changed even though you have, but the way is still open for you to repent."

Now, though, Jesus announces that one of the twelve would betray Him (13:18, 21). There is no indication in this scene that any among the twelve suspected Judas of treachery. No one pointed the finger at Judas and said, "He's the one." Instead, each of them asked, "Is it I?" But Jesus knew, for God knows the innermost thoughts of our hearts.

It is likely Judas was reclining immediately to Jesus's left—close enough for them to converse without the others hearing all that was said, for we read now that as Jesus handed Judas the sop, or morsel, He sent him on his way (13:27). The others there still did not understand what was happening, but John writes that Judas left the room immediately and then adds, "It was night" (13:30, KJV). This rather sinister note has to be symbolic of the night that was in Judas's soul as he turned his back on the One who came to be the "Light of the world" and went to perform his dastardly deed.

The fact that Jesus anticipated the Cross as His glorification (13:31–32) proves that for Him the redemption of the world through His coming death was His highest mission! And His words that "God shall also glorify him in himself" (13:32, KJV) express His total confidence in God and identification with Him.

In this farewell message of Jesus to His disciples He now gives them a farewell commandment. "A new command I give you: Love one another. As I have loved you, so you must love one another" (13:34, NIV). On the surface it might seem rather strange that Jesus now refers to this as a *new* commandment when even in the Old Testament we are admonished to love our neighbors as ourselves (Leviticus 19:18). But He does add a new dimension when He says, "As I have loved you." Jesus's love, opening Himself to us, is to the extent of death.

If we love others as He loves us, we will open ourselves to others to meet their needs whatever the cost to us! This then becomes the proof of our discipleship; our expression of love reflects His love. And by this love—not by our words, our doctrine, our traditions—the world will recognize that we know Jesus.

A vivid illustration of love's cost is seen in the story of Mary C. Funk, a young Mennonite woman who was returning many years ago to America on furlough from mission work in India. She first sailed from India to England and then boarded the *Titanic* for America. When the ship struck an iceberg and was sinking, Mary Funk was soon safely aboard a lifeboat. But then as she looked out across the deck, she saw a young woman clutching a child to her breast. Since the lifeboat was filled, Mary Funk got out and gave her place to the woman and child.

From the Gospels we've learned that Jesus's method of teaching in parables was very effective, and sometimes rather than tell a story He gave a parabolic statement. That is what He did here when, in response to Peter's question, "'Lord, where are you going?' Jesus replied, 'Where I am going, you cannot follow now, but you will follow later'" (13:36, NIV). Then Peter's question for clarity led to his assertion that he was willing to die for Jesus. There can be no doubt about Peter's sincerity at the moment, but Jesus knew of his weakness and said, "Before the rooster crows, you will disown me three times!" (13:38, NIV). And while John doesn't mention it here, we are reminded that in Luke, Jesus told Peter that "Satan demanded to have you, that he might sift you like wheat, but I have prayed for you that your faith may not fail" (Luke 22:31–32 ESV).

In spite of the fact that we, like Peter, don't fully understand ourselves and our faith is often shaky, we can take courage in the truth that Jesus doesn't give up on us any more than He did with Peter.

Fellowship—in Jesus as the Way

What is God like? This is the question that has intrigued many great minds throughout human history. It is answered simply in the verses we turn our attention to now (14:1–14). God is like Jesus. "Whoever has seen me has seen the Father" (14:9, ESV).

Jesus not only brought us the Good News. He *is* the Good News of the gospel. In our lesson now He proclaims boldly, "I am the way, and the truth, and the life; no one comes to the Father except through Me" (14:6, NASB).

At the very beginning of this part of our Scripture lesson Jesus seeks to calm the hearts and minds of His disciples. They believe in God, now they are to believe in the Son who has open access to the Father and to the Father's house (14:1–3). Jesus assured His disciples then and us now that while He must be away for a time, He will come again (14:3) and escort us to our heavenly home. We don't know when He will return. It could be tomorrow, or not for another thousand years. It will happen when His plans and purposes are fulfilled.

Jesus concludes the discussion about seeing the Father and responds to Philip's question with the amazing claim, "I am in the Father and the Father is in me" (14:11, NIV). The validity of this claim is found in both Jesus's words and His actions. The lesson for us here is that as children of God—Christians in the modern world—when we open our lives completely to

God, His will can be done in and through us as we strive with Christ's help to do those things that please the Father.

Finally, we find in verses 13 and 14 a remarkable promise for us in prayer. But it is conditioned by two phrases: "that the Father may be glorified in the Son" and "ask me anything in my name" (ESV). Asking for our own glory violates the condition. Similarly, asking in our own name or claim rather than asking according to the name of Jesus invalidates His promise. He promises to answer, but in the same context in which He affirmed the oneness between Himself and the Father, a oneness, a unity, in which we are to participate. Unity is a sense of oneness in the fellowship of Christ.

Now, to understand fully what Jesus is saying in verses 13 and 14 we need to look again at verse 12—a promise that has often been misinterpreted. "They will do even greater things than these, because I am going to the Father" (14:12, NIV). It is the completion of Jesus's redemptive mission and His return to the Father that assures us of answers to prayer. It is the finished work of Christ that gives us full access to God! Believing in Jesus opens the way for us to participate in His work—the ongoing and redeeming Good News of salvation through Jesus Christ that crosses all class, racial, cultural, and national lines and builds up the "body of Christ" across the world through the transforming work of the Holy Spirit.

Fellowship—in the Presence of the Spirit

Fellowship means togetherness, a sense of belonging that is expressed in loving openness with one another. And now Jesus continues His teaching in this part of our lesson (14:15–31) by saying, "If you love Me"—if you keep your life open to Me—"you will keep My commandments" (verse 15, NASB). The true measure of our love for God is found in our obedience to Him and His will for our lives. Or, to put it another way, a continuous love for God is our best safeguard against disobedience.

The full meaning of this "safeguard" is expressed as the presence of the Holy Spirit. Consequently, Jesus now says that He will ask the Father to give us *another* Comforter, the Holy Spirit, "that he may abide with you for ever" (14:16, KJV). The Greek word translated in verse 16—"Helper" (ESV), "advocate" (NIV), "Counselor" (AMP), or "Comforter" (KJV)—is *parakletos*. The Greek word was often used in legal or judicial contexts, and it can mean "Intercessor," as the Amplified Version suggests—one who intercedes, who speaks on our behalf. The ESV's broad term "Helper" covers all of the bases because the Spirit helps us handle all circumstances of life. The Holy Spirit is the Father's Advocate with us as believers in Jesus. The Father's Advocate is the "Spirit of truth" (14:17, KJV) who will keep us from error, guide us into all truth, and give us spiritual insight that the world lacks (read 1 Corinthians 2:1–13).

In this marvelous passage that has brought reassurance and confidence to Christians for millennia, Jesus speaks of the Father, the Son, the Holy Spirit, the disciples, the world, and the prince of this world (Satan) as He rolls back the curtain on the deepest meanings of reconciliation. Jesus and the Father express the deepest "togetherness": "I am in my father" (14:20, KJV). Jesus and the disciples experience "togetherness":

"I will not leave you . . . I will come to you" (14:18, 19, 21, 23, KJV). The Holy Spirit and the disciples experience intimate "togetherness": "he dwells with you and will be in you" and "he will teach you all things" (14:17, 26, ESV). By implication, the body of Christ—the church—experiences a unity that the world does not know (14:21–24). And this fellowship transcends the power or influence of the "prince of this world" (verse 30, NIV), the devil, for he has no power over Christ. In fact, the clash with this "prince of the world," which came at the Cross, showed people of all time how authentically Jesus lived by the will of the Father. Christ's victory in love, even to death, would "unmask" principalities and powers so that we would have a choice between the way of the world and the life of Christ. (See Colossians 2:15.)

This emphasis on "togetherness" is now followed by Jesus's great gift of peace. "Peace I leave with you; my peace I give you. I do not give to you as the world gives. Do not let your hearts be troubled and do not be afraid" (14:27, NIV). The word for peace in this verse is *shalom*. *Shalom* was the traditional Jewish greeting that implied not just absence of conflict but total well-being. Jesus's peace is His gracious identification with us, the full well-being of our unity, our fellowship with the Father. He then goes on to emphasize that fellowship by a reference to His going to the Father, who is "greater than I" (14:28, KJV). In other words, Jesus is saying that our Father—God—is indeed everything we have seen in the Son but that there is much more to God than the incarnate Son has been free to express in the limitations of His humanness. (See Philippians 2:5–11.)

These particular words of Jesus are a part of His last teaching before His death, and this makes them especially meaningful to us. In this part of Jesus's last teaching before the Cross it is important for us to note the emphasis on love and obedience. These two words are not contradictory; they are actually complementary. When love is understood as opening one's life intimately to another, then love for God is obedience. When obedience is understood as an attitude before it is an act, then obedience to God is love. And when both are seen together in reconciliation, as relational, there is freedom from legalism of all kinds.

The practical good news from these words of Jesus is that He calls us into togetherness, into family. The family of God. We *belong*.

Fellowship—by Abiding in Christ

Jesus now gives us the parable of the vine (15:1–8). This parable of the believer's relation to Christ is personal, but it is also universal, for it employs a transcultural figure. In many countries the vine is known as the source of food and drink. As the expression "I heard it through the grapevine" attests, it is also a remarkable figure of communication. Jesus may have selected the symbol from the "Lord's Supper," which He had just instituted. Or He may have selected it because the vine was a symbol of Israel (Psalm 80) and was carved over the temple gate.

Jesus's listeners and John's early readers would have remembered Isaiah's description of Israel and Judah as the vineyard and vine of God (5:1–7). Here we see the vineyard as a disappointment to God. Jeremiah 2:21 says that the noble vine (representing Israel and Judah) He had planted had turned into a "degenerate" (ESV) and "corrupt, wild" (NIV) plant.

It is against this background that Jesus asserts boldly, "I am the true vine" (15:1, KJV). Then He adds immediately that "my Father is the vinedresser" (verse 1, ESV), and in verse 5 the picture is completed as Jesus says, "I am the vine; you are the branches" (NIV).

In cultivating fruit trees and vines, it is vitally important to trim the branches, for when they are left untrimmed, they have less vitality, and some die. In addition, when a vine or tree is not pruned, the fruit is of a much poorer quality, and sometimes there may not be any fruit at all. There is far greater risk in underpruning than in overpruning.

In this parable Jesus now compares the Father to the vinedresser or "gardener" (verse 1, NIV)—the one who cares for the vines and prunes them as needed. The point is that anything that stands in the way of our living fruitful lives must be pruned—removed—even though it might be painful. This reminds us of the words from Hebrews 12:6: "The Lord disciplines the one he loves" (NIV).

Jesus next tells us that when we live fruitful and productive lives, we honor and give glory to the Father (15:8), and, of course, this is the real evidence that we are truly Jesus's disciples. Significantly, if we turn to Galatians and read about the "fruit of the Spirit" (5:22, KJV), it is clear that this "fruit" is not expressed or practiced in private but is seen in our relationships with others. Ours is not a faith of isolation but must be expressed in our day-to-day lives with family and "neighbors" near and far.

But the key to bearing fruit for God—for living productive and fruitful Christian lives—is possible only as we abide in Him. It is Christ's life in us that bears the fruit. Just as the sap of the vine flows into the branches to give life to produce fruit, so it is the energy of Christ, the life of Christ, in us that produces fruitful lives.

Jesus also makes it clear that the promise of answered prayer (15:7) is conditioned by our abiding in Him as He gives us one of the great promises found in the Gospels: "If you abide in me, and my words abide in you, ask whatever you wish, and it will be done for you" (ESV). In other words, the branch that abides in the vine and participates in the vine-life—the Word of God—can ask for anything that extends the purpose of the vine and it shall be done.

Fellowship—in the Practice of Love

Our relationship with God is one of love more than of the law. Contrary to the impression of many Christians, the law was under love even in the Old Testament, for in the Ark of the Covenant (Exodus 25:10–22) the tables of the law were kept *under* the Mercy Seat. Salvation has always been by God's mercy, by God's forgiving grace, not by adherence to the law. And yet one who lives in God's love lives in devotion to His will or His law. Psalm 119 is a remarkable testimony to this, for in all but two of its 176 verses there is a loving reference to the laws of God.

Jesus has opened for us a new understanding of this love-level of relationship with God, and now in this part of our lesson (15:9–17) He builds on this truth. "As the Father has loved me"—totally, unreservedly, in full identification with Him—"so have I loved you"—totally, unreservedly, in full identification with us (verse 9, NIV). And having said that, Jesus commands us to "remain in My love" (verse 10, NASB)—a call for us to maintain a total, full identification with Him at all times. Jesus then explains that to keep His commandments, to do His will, is to abide in His love (15:10).

In this marvelous lesson on the love theme we learn that the fellowship of love is
- the way to joy, the joy of belonging;
- response-love, the experience initiated by Jesus;
- self-giving, even to the extent of death (15:13);
- friendship at the deepest level of loyalty.

Life in Christ—the Good News of the gospel—is an expression of the commandment to love: first, to love God with our whole selves, and second, to love others as we love ourselves. And this great commandment is underlined here as Jesus says, ". . . love one another, as I have loved you" (15:12, KJV)—totally, unreservedly, even to the point of dying for us. Jesus then builds on this great love theme by elevating the position of His disciples and us to that of friends. "You are my friends if you do what I command you. No longer do I call you servants . . . but I have called you friends" (15:14–15, ESV). We are His friends as we live in His love. And this friendship makes us full partners in His mission. What a marvelous truth! You and I are in partnership with Jesus Christ.

The initiative of divine grace is expressed in Jesus's words when He says, "You did not choose me, but I chose you" (15:16, NIV). At the time, these words, of course, had primary meaning for the twelve disciples, but their greater meaning includes you and me. Our faith does not originate with a blind search for God but is our response to God, who has chosen us to live fruitful—fruit-bearing—lives and at the same time has given us assurance that whatever we ask in His name, in His purpose, the Father will give us. This is His promise to us as members of the family of God.

Again, in verse 17 Jesus repeats the commandment to "love one another" (KJV). This is the third time He has stressed this theme in these verses, for the heart of the ethic of discipleship is love. The third epistle of John expands at length on this theme in the third and fourth chapters. Here, with apparent reference to Jesus's own words in our Gospel lesson, John writes, "And this is his commandment, that we believe in the name of his Son Jesus Christ and love one another, just as he has commanded us. . . . And this commandment we have from him: whoever loves God must also love his brother" (1 John 3:23; 4:21, ESV).

And how do we love one another? In 1 John 3:18 we find our answer: "Dear children, let us not love with words or speech but with actions and in truth" (NIV).

Fellowship—in Separation from the World

In these closing verses of our lesson (15:18–27) Jesus drives home the point that while His disciples in all times are in the world, we are not "of the world" (15:19, ESV). Our citizenship is in heaven (Philippians 3:20). We are, first of all, members of the Kingdom of God. And contrary to what seems to happen all too often, we are to build up and encourage our brothers and sisters in Christ even though at times their understanding of what Jesus would do in a given situation may differ from ours. This is what is involved in loving one another.

At the same time Jesus warns the disciples that the world will reject and hate them even as it does Him. The Christian's identification with Christ is an affront to the world. The same spirit that rejects Jesus rejects those who identify with Him.

In the first centuries of the church, in the Roman Empire, every citizen was expected to offer a "pinch of incense" and say, "Caesar is lord." Then when that little ritual was out of the way, they could serve any god they chose at a secondary level to Caesar. But the Christians refused to do this, and they were hated and hounded and even martyred for saying simply, "Jesus is Lord!" They refused to in any way compromise in their commitment to Christ even though the cost of their separation from the world was high.

But our separation as Christians is not first and foremost *from* the world, it is *to* Christ. By being committed to Jesus we will be selective about all other commitments. "The servant is not greater than his lord" (15:20, KJV), so consequently, as we are faithful to God in our witness, we can expect rejection and opposition.

That opposition is equally present today even though it may take different forms. For some, it is not being accepted by the "in group" or losing friendships or opportunities because of their faith. For others, the danger may be in the form of emotional and psychological repression. And there are those even today who face prison and bodily harm because they refuse to offer their "pinch of incense."

The presence of Christ exposed the sin of the world (15:22), and this is most clearly revealed at Calvary. At the Cross the world said in effect, "We'd rather get rid of God than serve Him," for to reject Jesus was, and is, to reject God.

We have seen in this lesson that our role as Christians is to be in fellowship first with God through Jesus Christ and then with one another. We are to love as we are loved, and we are to be witnesses in society of the family of God. And it is our witness to Christ that brings about our separation from the world. Jesus foresaw all of this, and now in verse 26 He again promises the Comforter—our Advocate and Intercessor and Helper—the Holy Spirit who is given to enable and secure our witness. As members of the family of God, we are called to be the light of the world, punching holes in the darkness.

Thank You for the ministry of the Holy Spirit in my life. He guides me when I need direction; comforts me when I grieve; and encourages me to live for You. AMEN.

INSPIRATION FROM THE GOSPEL OF JOHN

"Peace I leave with you; my peace I give you. I do not give to you as the world gives. Do not let your hearts be troubled and do not be afraid."

—John 14:27 (NIV)

One of my summer highlights was attending a weeklong Bible camp in Washington state with my two daughters and their husbands. Each morning there was a program that included a chapel service that began with a half hour of singing.

One morning we sang "It Is Well with My Soul": "When peace, like a river, attendeth my way, / When sorrows like sea billows roll, / Whatever my lot, Thou hast taught me to know, / It is well, it is well, with my soul."

The songwriter, Horatio G. Spafford, was a successful lawyer and real estate investor. In 1871 the Great Chicago Fire destroyed his downtown properties. Two years later his four young daughters drowned at sea. In the midst of unimaginable pain, Spafford—a follower of Jesus—penned these lyrics as his testimony. His words have blessed millions, reminding us that we, too, can know peace in the midst of life's storms, because Jesus is with us.

The guitars and keyboard fell silent as the camp worship leader led us into the final chorus. Four-part harmony filled the auditorium. When the song ended, no one moved. No one spoke a word. Christ's presence hung over the room like the glory of God filled the Temple in Old Testament days. I wish I could have bottled the moment. I reflect often on that morning, and my heart breaks into song.

Thanks be to Jesus for the gift of shalom peace. Wholeness, completeness, harmony, and tranquility of soul is ours because of who He is and what He's done for us.

—*Grace Fox*

Notes

Notes

Notes

LESSON 6: JOHN 16–17

Christ the Reconciler— in Unity

Lord, help me learn this lesson and pass on to others what I learn. AMEN.

The family of God is a new community reconciled in Christ. With a diversity of culture, race, class, personality, and every facet of humanity, we are united in one body as the people of God. The twelve disciples are an example of this oneness, this quality of unity. No one but Jesus could enable Simon the Zealot and Matthew the tax collector to walk as brothers! No one but Jesus could unite James and John, the sons of thunder, and Andrew, the caring enabler. Jesus is creating a new people that are united around Him.

Unity—through the Work of the Spirit

Knowing as He did what lay ahead for His disciples in the way of testing and persecution, Jesus now speaks to the importance of their unity in the Spirit (16:1–16). It is through the work of God's Spirit in our lives that we have the boldness to confront possible persecution and even death, and not only confront that fear, but overcome it. For just as with the Spirit's help we overcome our fear of death, we will at the same time overcome our fear of life. This is important in our daily walk as Christians, for if we live under the fear of failure and death, we are unable to assume the risks of living boldly for God.

The disciples are warned here that they may be isolated and put out of the synagogues—banned from their customary places of worship—but their unity with God through the Holy Spirit will take them through their times of trial. Jesus spoke to the fear of persecution and death by setting it in the larger context of the Kingdom of the Father in conflict with the kingdoms of this world. And He could speak of going to the Father with such joy that leaving this world was relegated to its proper place—accepted but not courted (16:1–6).

The ultimate meaning of the Kingdom of God is the presence and rule of God among us. Jesus, anticipating His coming departure (16:5), now gives some very significant and pointed teaching about the coming of the Holy Spirit, God's other Presence. In saying, "It is expedient for you that I go away" (16:7, KJV), we come to understand Christ's awareness that while His presence localizes God in Jesus of Nazareth, His physical departure from this earth would permit God's universal presence in the person of the Holy Spirit. Earlier Jesus had said that He would ask the Father, and He would send the Spirit to the disciples. But now Jesus says, "I will send him unto you" (verse 7, KJV). Here we see the basis of the line in the Nicene Creed that says that "the Holy Spirit . . . proceeds from the Father and the Son."

The Spirit's presence is God's presence, extending His rule in the world through those who are open to Him. In these

verses, we see a clear outline of the three things Jesus said the Spirit will do:
1) He will convince the world of sin because they believe not, by showing the world faith through *our* believing (verse 8).
2) He will convince the world of righteousness after Jesus has returned to the Father by the witness of *our* righteous lives (verse 9).
3) He will convince the world of judgment by showing that Satan is judged and defeated now in our lives as we witness to freedom (verse 11).

We come to understand here that the Spirit is God's supervisory agent in the ongoing life and direction of the church. He enriches the church by
1) guiding us into all truth (verse 13);
2) glorifying Christ in us (verse 14); and
3) taking of the grace of Christ and sharing it with us (verse 15).

Jesus told the disciples in all times that the Holy Spirit "will not speak on his own authority" (16:13, ESV). In other words, He will not speak independent of the Father and the Son, but He will impart and illuminate the revelation of the Father in the Son.

Jesus now assures the disciples that although He will be leaving them physically, they will see Him again (16:16). And this remains our hope as we look and work expectantly for His second coming.

Jesus's teaching here on unity in the Spirit carries important overtones for us today. It is essential that we not become so preoccupied with our understanding or form or interpretation of the faith that we become belligerent and critical of our brothers and sisters in Christ. Rather, we should devote our time and energies to understanding God's Word and developing a worldview based upon it. For the Holy Spirit inspired the Word, and He will illuminate our minds to understand it. This is the same Spirit that calls us to Christ, and as we are open to Him, He will transform us into the likeness of Christ.

Unity—in the Spirit of Joy

In response to the questions that raged in the disciples' minds, Jesus now turns His attention to that quality of joy that is the believer's birthright, which transcends any temporary separation or time of sorrow (16:17–24). He wants His disciples and us to see that joy is a relational experience. It is a "high" of belonging, of fellowship. Joy is holistic, for it is a matter of spirit and affects the whole of life. It has dimensions of anticipation, of participation, and of fulfillment. The writer of the epistle to the Hebrews says of Jesus, "Who for the joy that was set before him endured the cross, despising the shame, and is set down at the right hand of the throne of God" (Hebrews 12:2, KJV).

Joy is an atmosphere of acceptance, of goodwill, of being participants in something of "meaning." By its very spirit, joy unifies; it binds us together at the spiritual level of life. As Christians, we are united in worship and praise. We find this expressed a little later in the Gospel as Jesus shares His joy in His oneness with the Father and in turn invites us into oneness with Him (17:20–23). And as we experience that oneness—that unity with God the Father and with Jesus—the joy of the Lord dominates all of life. As Sam Shoemaker (1893–1963), a noted speaker and minister of the early twentieth century, once said, "The surest mark of a Christian is not faith, or even love, but joy."

But this experience of transitional thinking was not easy for the disciples. They were too close to the woods to see the trees. Because they were still expecting His Kingdom to be a sociopolitical rule that would subdue their enemies, they did not yet see the Kingdom of God as a Messianic order that is primarily spiritual and ethical. This was an ongoing struggle for the disciples, and because of it they were often uncertain about Jesus. Jesus knew there could be no joy in uncertainty. Joy is interfaced with assurance. And so by His words and actions He provided this assurance.

Hundreds of years before, Nehemiah had captured the power and attractiveness of joy when he said, "The joy of the Lord is your strength" (Nehemiah 8:10, KJV). It is with the spirit of joy that we achieve strength and unity and become appealing and winsome witnesses of the gospel of Christ.

We see also in our study that Jesus's words of assurance (16:19–24) to His disciples are given in the context of His anticipation of His coming death. His comment about their grief that would turn to joy implies His full awareness of the Cross and the Resurrection.

Then in verse 21, when He likened His death and resurrection to travail and birth, He was looking ahead to the beginning of the new age, a time of full reconciliation with the Father. While the disciples did not completely understand what Jesus meant by all of this at the time, there is no doubt that the full meaning of His promises came to them after the Cross and empty tomb were realities. In a similar way, the meanings of many biblical passages become clear to us only after we have personally entered into their meaning. It is then that the spirit of rejoicing enriches our lives, and His special joy becomes the witness and radiance of the gospel.

The privilege of full reconciliation is ours in Christ. We can look up and say, "Abba, Father; I'm one of Your children, and I have access to the throne!" And in that confidence we have the amazing promise that "my Father will give you whatever you ask in my name. Until now you have not asked for anything in my name. Ask and you will receive, and your joy will be complete" (16:23–24, NIV). There is no partial measure promised here. Our joy is complete because through Jesus Christ we're able to have audience with God the Father Himself.

Unity—in a Community of Faith

Each community of people has its origins in at least one shared, common characteristic. For some it is class, for others it is economic interests or political views, and for some it is values or racial or cultural identity. But for the disciples of Jesus Christ, our focus is a faith relationship with God the Father. Even so, within the Christian church we are often divided by the same diversity of focus that fragments the world. And yet we know there is no Christian culture as such. No single group or denomination has captured the Kingdom! And no nationalism has an edge on the grace of God.

But as we turn our attention to Jesus's words now (16:25–33), three things stand out:
1) We are in God's love when we are in Jesus's love. (16:27)
2) We need to understand Jesus if we are to have an intelligent faith. (16:29–30)
3) Jesus has overcome the world and enabled us to have "peace" and "good cheer." (16:32–33)

Jesus came from the Father and entered the world, and having made that major adjustment, He now viewed His death and resurrection as the next adjustment to return to the Father. And the great affirmation that comes to us is that just as Jesus faced death in full confidence that the Father would raise Him up, so we face death in full confidence in Jesus's promise to raise us up!

The community of Jesus is a community of faith. In his letter to the Ephesian Christians, Paul asserted that there is "one Lord, one faith, one baptism, one God and Father of all, who is above all, and through all, and in you all" (Ephesians 4:5–6, KJV). We are initiated by Jesus into *one* community of faith. Jesus entered the world to create this special people. The mission of the church—our community of faith—is to offer the broken and lonely people in today's world a *new community* in Christ. And He reconciles us to Himself to be this people, promising that "in me you may have peace" (16:33, ESV). And He assures us of victory as His people, for even in the face of impending death Jesus says, "I have overcome the world" (16:33, ESV).

The powers of evil in the world killed His body, but they did not crush His spirit, for on the third day He was victorious over death. And even as the world could not defeat Jesus, it cannot defeat us—our victory is a matter of spirit just as His was. It is seen in our joy and peace, which do not depend upon what happens *to* us but what happens *within* us. This peace resides in us and produces an inner harmony that radiates our joy and witnesses to our community with God. Jesus *is* our peace. And faith unites us to Him and permits Him to be Himself *in us*!

Unity—in Personal Prayer

There is nothing that expresses the true spirit of one's life the way prayer does. When we address God, it becomes clear just how well we know Him, how honest we are with Him, and how we seek to relate to Him. Self-interests show up immediately in our prayers. Reverence, or lack of it, is evident in our prayers. In fact, prayer reveals who is actually in charge of our lives. Frequently it seems that the one praying is really "in charge" and is merely attempting to use God as a cosmic concierge.

But true prayer is communion with God; it is not talking God into doing something. And it is certainly not overcoming God's reluctance or attempting to "twist God's arm." Rather, prayer is laying hold of God's willingness. It is conditioning ourselves to God's will so that He has the moral freedom to carry out what He has been wanting to do for some time but for which He had to await our participation.

Jesus's prayer in the seventeenth chapter of John is the ultimate example of true reverence and communion with God. First, in the opening verses (17:1–5) we discover that the personal base of prayer is in the privilege of addressing God as "Father," for the purpose in prayer is that He should be glorified (17:1). And the priorities of personal prayer are established so that we can fulfill the work God has asked us to do (17:4). This is the highest priority for every day of our lives—to finish the work God has given us to do for that day.

Then, too, we learn that prayer follows the "laws" of divine grace. There are laws of gravity, laws of seasons (we don't plant corn in December), and laws of relationship. These laws of prayer must not be broken, for prayer does not misuse God. Rather it conforms us to the will of God.

Prayer is also the clearest expression of the character of our theology. We tend to complicate things with lengthy and involved explanations and arguments about biblical and doctrinal aspects of our understanding of God. But we would do well to heed the attitude of Dr. Karl Barth, the famous Swiss theologian. When asked to share the greatest thought that ever crossed his mind, he answered after a brief pause, "Jesus loves me, this I know, for the Bible tells me so."

In the opening lines of Jesus's prayer we are given in simple and understandable form the interpretation of eternal life: "And this is eternal life, that they may know You, the only true God, and Jesus Christ whom You have sent" (17:3, NASB). Building on this interpretation, the Westminster Confession states that our primary purpose as Christians is "to glorify God and to *enjoy Him forever*" (italics added for emphasis).

We also find in these opening personal words—"And now, Father, glorify me in your own presence with the glory that

I had with you before the world existed" (17:5, ESV)—that Jesus was looking ahead to the agony of the Cross. The extent of Jesus's commitment to our salvation is conveyed here as He sees the Cross as the expression of the glory of God's grace. And we see Jesus's great integrity of purpose as He uses the authority God had given Him to serve us, to give us eternal life, here and forever. But Jesus didn't pray for His disciples and us only then—He continues to pray for us now. Paul underlined this truth when he wrote, "Christ Jesus who died—more than that, who was raised to life—is at the right hand of God and is also interceding for us" (Romans 8:34, NIV).

Unity—in Prayer for Disciples

"Hear, O Israel: The LORD our God is one . . . ." These words from Deuteronomy 6:4 (KJV) are known as the *Shema* and are at the heart of the Judaic-Christian understanding of God. By "one" we mean "oneness"—not a mathematical or numerical one. Jesus shows us who God is. Jesus says, "The one who has seen Me has seen the Father" (John 14:9, NASB). And now as Jesus prays for His disciples (17:6–12), He says, "I have manifested Your name [and revealed Your very self, Your real self] to the people whom You have given Me out of the world" (17:6, AMP).

At the same time, Jesus expresses the nature of divine initiative in calling out a people of God. It is God who moves *to* us in grace. The initiative is with Him. This is the unique difference between Christianity and the other religions of the world. While the others are involved in a search to find God, salvation by grace through Jesus Christ means that God has taken the initiative and has come to us. So Jesus in this prayer sees His disciples, and us, as a gift of God to Him. Paul elaborated on this truth when he wrote the Ephesian Christians and explained that we are Christ's inheritance (Ephesians 1:18). We are His people; we belong to Him (John 17:7–8).

This is a marvelous truth that we can and should claim every day of our lives. The twenty-first-century world is increasingly complex in both relationships and technology. The rumblings of war and conflict fill the news. The epidemics of opioid addiction and suicide bring to the surface our feelings of inability to cope. But even in the midst of such challenges, we are told in this prayer of Jesus that we are His! And as members of His fellowship of believers, we are assured that in His power we can handle anything that comes our way.

In verse 9 Jesus makes it clear that He is praying for His disciples and not for the world. His prayer now is for the people who follow Him—who go out to win the world in Jesus's name. Then He makes a statement that would be audacious if He were not the Son of God: "All things that are Mine are Yours, and Yours are Mine" (17:10, NASB). Next He asks the Father to protect the disciples "by the power of your name, the name you gave me" (verse 11, NIV). And finally, He prays that His disciples "may be one" as the Father and Son are one (17:11, NASB).

Jesus and the Father can be seen as one in *purpose*—"I have [finished] the work you gave me to do" (17:4, NIV); in *mutual honor*—"Glorify your Son, that your Son may glorify you" (17:1, NIV); and in full *partnership*—"All things that are Mine are Yours, and [all things that are] Yours are Mine" (17:10, AMP). And the oneness to which Jesus calls us is to be of the same character. It is not a surface unity but a deep sense of togetherness in the reconciling grace of God.

Prayer makes us partners. We are participants in God's work. In some places across the United States, immense pipelines are laid to carry oil from the oil fields to refineries many miles away. But in order for these pipelines to function, pumping stations every 30 miles are necessary to push the oil along to its ultimate destination. As partners in God's work in our world, our task is similar to those pumping stations, for as we share with one another, we are carrying the good work of God's love and grace along.

Unity—in Prayer for Sanctity

Holiness means that we belong completely to God, that we are wholly His. The consequence or subjective aspect of holiness or sanctification is wholeness, the correcting of our perversions and the healing of our broken selves. It is this brokenness or self-centeredness that is the basic obstacle to oneness. Hence, Jesus's prayer for oneness moves to the plea for His disciples to be sanctified by the Truth (17:13–19).

Jesus begins by telling us that it is through a wholistic relationship with the Father that we experience the full joy of Christ (17:13). This is the joy of belonging, of assurance, of being God's own possession. As such, we are not of the world but members of the family of God. Twice in these verses Jesus says that His disciples are not of the world, just as He is not of the world (17:14, 16). At the same time, though, we understand that Jesus did not pray for His disciples to be taken out of the world (17:15). Christianity is not an escape or an otherworldly religion. Instead, we have the promise of victory through Christ in the ordinary and everyday affairs of life.

Perhaps our best example is that of Jesus, who was *in* the world but not *of* it. He was with people, healing, helping, encouraging. We, too, are called as He was to be agents of reconciliation, to be healers—ambassadors of Christ (2 Corinthians 5:19–20). We are extensions of the presence of Christ, witnesses for Him in our world today. And witnessing is done by presence, service, and communication—in that order.

In verse 17 we find a very important petition in Jesus's prayer, "Sanctify them in the truth; your word is truth" (17:17, ESV). The truth of God is expressed in the Word of God—the Word made flesh, that is Jesus, and the Word taught and written. In the written Word that is inspired by the Spirit we meet the Christ, the Word personified. And in Jesus we are meeting God. He is the Word, the revealer of God (17:2). It is this truth that calls us, that sets us apart as God's people, that sanctifies or makes us holy.

This part of our lesson closes now as Jesus identifies with His disciples when He says, "And for their sakes I sanctify myself, that they also might be sanctified through the truth" (17:19, KJV). In other words, Jesus sets Himself apart from the world of self-interest to be wholly God's person. And in so doing Jesus opens the way through the Cross for us to become fully and totally God's persons as well. We are set apart in unity with Him to live whole and productive lives.

Unity—in Prayer for All who Believe

Futuristic prayer is one's belief in the ongoing work of God. He is the main actor on the stage of history, carrying out His work. We pray believing that He continues to work. In our time, despite world hunger, violence, and the nuclear threat, we can still pray, believing that God's providential care assures a future for this world.

Jesus prayed not only for those with whom He had shared His life but for all who would come to believe in Him down through the thousands of years (17:20–26). He prayed for you and me. He prayed that we might be one with Him and the Father. Notice the expression ". . . that they also may be one *in us*" (17:21, KJV; italics added for emphasis). We also are to be one, along with the disciples who composed His immediate group. This oneness is a unity of persons and purpose in the midst of our diversity.

The heart of Jesus's prayer for all future believers is the prayer for oneness (17:21–23). The body of Christ is one, and the diversity of its parts is not a division in the body. With all of our cultural and philosophical conditioning that separates us into so many denominations, we must avoid idolizing any theological group and see ourselves as a part of the church universal, the one body of Christ.

The unity for which Jesus prayed is not structurally or institutionally negotiated. Rather it is a reconciliation of Spirit, a being made mature in oneness (17:23). And this oneness, which transcends our self-centeredness, becomes a primary witness to the world of the reconciling grace of God (17:21, 23).

Now as Jesus concludes this prayer, we are reminded again of the early verses of the Gospel (1:1–3). Jesus refers to His relationship with the Father in love "before the foundation of the world" (17:24, KJV). This relates directly to the opening words of the Gospel, "In the beginning was the Word . . . . All things were made by him" (1:1, 3, KJV)

The prayer closes with Jesus's summation of salvation: that we might know the Father through Him, and that God's love might be in us and Christ in us. Paul worded it this way when he wrote to the Colossian Christians, "Christ *in you,* the hope of glory" (Colossians 1:27, KJV; italics added for emphasis).

Merciful Father, help me to sow peace, love, joy, and unity among Your followers. AMEN.

INSPIRATION FROM THE GOSPEL OF JOHN

"These things I have spoken to you so that My joy may be in you, and that your joy may be made full. This is My commandment, that you love one another, just as I have loved you."

—John 15:11–12 (NASB)

While watering the flower box on our front porch, the spray suddenly stopped. I squeezed the handle more firmly, checked the setting, and wiggled the hose. Finally I found a kink in the line that had stopped the water from flowing. Once I untangled the hose, the water sprayed freely, and I was able to finish watering my flowers and herbs.

There are times when joy seems like a meager drip in my life, even though I know Jesus promises to give it in abundance. When I realize that I've stopped raining joy on those around me, it's a good signal for me to check for blockages and tangles. Jesus linked His promise of joy with His command to love others in the same way He loved. Often when my joy dries up, I discover that

I've begun to focus so much on my own needs or hurts that I've stopping letting Jesus's love for others flow through me. The knot grows tighter, my spirit shrivels, and I have nothing to pour out into the lives of others.

My first response when I recognize lack of joy in my heart is to try harder. Like twisting the nozzle or squeezing more intensely, this does no good if I'm not open to the Source. I need to remind myself that I can run to Jesus, ask Him to change my heart, to live in me, to connect me to the Source of joy, so I can love others as He does.

Like the generous spray that waters my flowers, joy flows naturally when He forgives the sins that block our relationship. Because of Him, we can open our hearts to His love again and overflow with joy.

—*Sharon Hinck*

Notes

Notes

Notes

LESSON 7: JOHN 18–19

Christ the Reconciler— in Love

Father God, teach me to serve You with Christlike conviction. Edify me with Your Word. AMEN.

Love is a depth of caring that opens one's life fully to that of another. We read earlier in our Gospel account that God so loved the world that He gave His only begotten Son. That kind of love calls for a response of love on our part. We love Him because He first loved us (1 John 4:19). And now, because we are His disciples, His love is poured into our lives through the Holy Spirit (Romans 5:5). If love was possible without the gospel, we wouldn't need the gospel. On the other hand, if love is not possible through the gospel, we have no gospel. But the truth is that love is made possible by the gospel, and that is what Christian discipleship is all about!

Love—that Doesn't Resist

John tells us now that when the meal was over, Jesus and His disciples left the upper room and walked the short distance across the Kidron brook to the Garden of Gethsemane, a place they often frequented. One can't help but wonder why Jesus didn't go someplace where He wouldn't be so easily found since He knew He was going to be betrayed and arrested. But authentic love doesn't run. Rather, it participates in love without reacting to the way it's treated. Jesus's kind of love could confront hostility without becoming hostile in return (18:1–11). In fact, the depth of Jesus's love is seen in His suffering and death.

How far short of this most of us come. It is easier to respond to anger with anger, to violence with violence. Turning the other cheek, being free to respond differently from the way in which we have been treated, takes an inner strength from God's grace. Yet this is the Christian's strategy of operation.

John relates Judas's betrayal by plainly identifying him with the enemies of Jesus. Judas was a child of this world, and he failed to embrace the Kingdom of God that Jesus had announced. By betraying Jesus he chose the way of coercion and violence rather than the way of freedom and love seen in Jesus.

Jesus's composure, courage, and boldness before the mob were a reflection of His own inner peace and authority (18:4–8). He knew who He was, and one who stands in truth and love is not vulnerable before deceit and violence.

In this scene John does not report on Judas's act of identifying Jesus with a kiss (Matthew 26:47–50 and Mark 14:43–45), but instead shows us Jesus's fearless demeanor before the mob. They had been led to the Garden of Gethsemane by Judas. He knew that this part of the garden was Jesus's place of prayer and rest. It was here that the dramatic confrontation took place, and as Jesus identified Himself, John writes that the mob fell back to the earth (18:6), a sign of the power Jesus had—a power that could have been used for His escape had He so chosen. But love does not run from trouble, and Jesus's selfless love was expressed in His appeal that the mob would let His disciples alone (18:8).

Next John describes Peter's impulsive action. He drew his sword and cut off the ear of the high priest's servant, Malchus. John takes particular care to tell us it was his "right ear." This could mean that Peter was a poor swordsman, or that the servant turned his head at just the right moment, or perhaps Peter was left-handed. One wonders at the specificity, except that it relates the story in a simplistic form. But of far more importance is Jesus's rebuke to Peter. "Put your sword away! Shall I not drink the cup the Father has given me?" (18:11, NIV). Jesus made it clear that He was completely submissive to the Father's will.

On one of his Thracian campaigns, Julius Caesar captured Spartacus the gladiator. He sent him to the arena to fight an unknown opponent. As Spartacus entered the arena, he spoke a phrase that was peculiar to the area where his boyhood home was located. In a flash his opponent responded with an equally familiar phrase. Suddenly Spartacus realized he was standing toe to toe with his younger brother! He threw his short sword across the arena, reached out and jerked the helmet from his brother's head, and kissed him on the cheek. Calling out to Caesar he said, "Sir, we fight not, for we are brothers." As Christians reconciled in love with our brothers and sisters across the world, our response to the people and situations in life is to be like that of Jesus in the garden— boldly determined in peace to do the Father's will.

It was there—in the garden under the full moon of the Passover just hours before His death—that Jesus showed us the *better way*: the way of life and victory.

Love—under Test

The trial of Jesus was really the exposure of the human family (18:12–27). To reject such a one as Jesus of Nazareth meant a choice for evil against God. And the choice was made by the Jewish religious community as well as by the secular/political community. This is highlighted by the fact that Jesus was taken before both Annas, retired high priest, and then his son-in-law, Caiaphas, the current high priest (18:13–14).

John makes special note of the prediction given by Caiaphas to the Jewish leaders: "It was expedient that one man should die for the people" (18:14, KJV), a repeat of a prophecy he had made earlier (11:51). Most certainly these words originated not from his piety but by virtue of his position. Here is a prime example of the kind of person who has a head knowledge of religion but is totally lacking in spiritual and moral perception.

We are told next that Peter and "another disciple" followed Jesus to the high priest's house. Tradition holds that this other disciple was John, identified as the writer of this Gospel, who was apparently acquainted with the high priest and had access to his palace. Such being the case, it appears clear that the detailed account of the events told here is not secondhand. It also tells us something about John's social acceptance in

Jerusalem society. It is thought that Zebedee had a house in Jerusalem from which he marketed salt fish and supplied the house of Caiaphas. Peter's easy access was due to John's friendship, as it was John who interceded with the maid at the door and secured Peter's entrance into the palace itself (18:15–16).

The stories of Peter's denial and of Jesus's interrogation are interspersed in John's account of what happened. In this we see a sharp contrast between Peter's weakness and Jesus's strength. As the high priest asked Jesus about His disciples and His doctrine (18:19–21), the two visible aspects of His program and influence, Jesus answered fearlessly and directly. And when one of the officers took exception to the directness of Jesus's response, he "struck Jesus with the palm of his hand" (18:22, KJV) even though He was bound (18:24). In turn Jesus gave a bold rebuke to the officer who struck him (18:23). We see in Jesus's words and actions here that love is not weak, and it holds people accountable.

The account of Peter's denial of Jesus (18:17–18; 25–27) exposes not only Peter's weakness but ours as well, along with our tendency to self-preservation at any cost. Many of us meet ourselves in Peter. So often we find ways to compromise for self-interest rather than accept the cost of love. The late Dr. E. Stanley Jones, a prominent missionary and preacher, mentioned three basic areas of temptation: the self drive, the social drive, and the sex drive. In the story of Peter's denial it is possible that all three of these converged in one experience. Peter denied his Lord—the most important person in his life—under the social and self-preservation pressures of the young women servants of the palace and of the soldiers who had arrested Jesus.

Compromise tends to accelerate. Peter's first denial made the second more emphatic, and his third was accompanied by an oath. It is possible that John's respect for his erring friend is reflected in the matter-of-fact, nonjudgmental way in which he tells the story.

John doesn't give us the final scene of Peter's denial. In the Gospel of Luke, as soon as the rooster crowed, "The Lord turned and looked straight at Peter" (Luke 22:61, NIV). That loving look accomplished far more than any reprimand, for Peter "went outside and wept bitterly" (Luke 22:62, NIV). This marks the difference between Peter and Judas. The latter would not repent and come back to the Master.

Love is not a guarantee that we won't fail at times, but when we're put to the test, love calls us back.

Love—that Faces the Powers

We come now to Jesus's infamous civil trial before Pilate, the Roman governor (18:28–40). While the conniving Jewish religious leaders were determined to see Jesus killed, we find a touch of irony in verse 28 because they refused to enter Pilate's judgment hall. In so doing they would have become "defiled" religiously. They had no scruples about manipulating events and stories so as to kill an innocent man, but they didn't want to break one of their "religious" rules.

Pilate didn't want to deal with Jesus (18:33–38). He wanted Jesus off his hands. But the leaders from the Sanhedrin made it clear that their "kangaroo court" wanted Jesus put to death. The verdict was already given—they only needed Pilate to authorize the execution. That's why they'd brought Jesus to the Fortress of Antonia to be tried by the Roman governor.

The interchange between Pilate and Jesus contains one of the most striking presentations in the Gospel. It is before the political authority that Jesus clearly states His kingship and the nature of His Kingdom. It is a kingdom of love, of freedom, of truth. It is a kingdom of peace, for Jesus said, "My kingdom is not of this world. If it were, my servants would fight to prevent my arrest by the Jewish leaders. But now my kingdom is from another place" (18:36, NIV). He wanted Pilate, the man of political authority and power, to know that He was talking about the Kingdom of God, not an earthly realm.

Pilate's response to Jesus's witness to truth was typical of the agnostic mind: "What is truth?" (18:38, NIV). In other words, who can be sure? How can we know? And yet the One who stood before him had said earlier, "I am the way, and the truth, and the life. No one comes to the Father except through me" (14:6, ESV). If we would know the truth of God, we must be open to be confronted by God! We can't handle the truth of God as an idea, or it is not the truth of God. A person can be known only in relationship.

Truth aims to teach people how to take sides. Truth is not neutrality, rather it produces the boldest and bravest of spirits. In Christ, God took sides—for us! And as Christians, as children of God, we can never back away from the responsibility of making spiritual decisions.

That Pilate could recognize the authenticity of Jesus's claims is seen in his attempt to negotiate His release (18:39). Significantly, here and on three other occasions Pilate said, "I find in him no fault at all" (18:38, KJV). His offer to release a prisoner was an attempt to get Jesus off, and the comparison of Jesus with Barabbas was a contrast between peace and violence, love and hostility, faith and force, service and theft. But the mob's choice of Barabbas (18:40) revealed the full character of their hostility, for their antagonism toward the Messiah and their desire to secure their own place of power was of the very spirit of Barabbas. They chose the kingdom of the world rather than the Kingdom of God.

Love—that Accepts Rejection

The Apostle's Creed reads, ". . . suffered under Pontius Pilate, was crucified . . . ." Our Scripture lesson now gives us in graphic terms the account of Jesus's complete rejection by the Jerusalem mob (19:1–16). First, Jesus is tied to the whipping post to be scourged—a Roman torture intended to weaken a victim before crucifixion. The scourging itself was done with a whip of leather thongs containing metal barbs that lacerated the flesh. Many persons collapsed under such scourging. In Jesus's case, the whipping was accompanied by the mockery of the soldiers who pressed a crown of thorns into His head and dressed Him in a purple robe. And this was followed by jeers and slaps and punches as they taunted Him about being King of the Jews (19:2–3).

Pilate's act of bringing the scourged, thorn-crowned Jesus out to the people was no doubt an attempt to satisfy the crowd that Jesus had been beaten. Stating again that he found no fault in Him, Pilate called upon the crowd to "Behold the man!" (ESV), hoping to now release Him (19:4–5). But the cry of the crowd, stirred up by the leaders, was "Crucify him, crucify him!" (19:6, ESV). What a contrast to the welcome given Him just a few days before, when Jesus had entered Jerusalem to the tumultuous cries, "Hosanna! Blessed is he who comes in the name of the Lord, even the King of Israel!" (John 12:13, ESV).

Now the accusation took up a new note. "He made Himself out to be the Son of God!" (19:7, NASB). It is significant that Pilate did not mock at this but took it seriously. He had been impressed by Jesus's person and presence. John writes, "He was even more afraid" (19:8, NASB). Even after all of this, Pilate took the beaten Jesus into the judgment hall and asked again who He was! And when Jesus didn't answer, Pilate tried to move Him to answer by a reference to his own Roman power (19:10).

In response to Pilate's assertion of power, Jesus now answered that He knew only one power—the power of God—and all other power was only that granted by God (19:11). In writing to the Roman Christians, Paul picks up on this same theme when he says, "For there is no power but of God: the powers that be are ordained of God" (Romans 13:1, KJV). God is always above the powers of this world.

The extent of the treachery and madness of the Jewish religious leaders was revealed now in how they responded to

Pilate's effort to release the innocent Jesus. In essence, they blackmailed him by saying he would be disloyal to Caesar if he let Jesus go (19:12). Pilate's tenure as governor had been marked by disastrous failure, but a charge of disloyalty to his emperor would have ruined him, so he caved in. Then after another scene in the judgment hall, Pilate stood Jesus before the mob and said, "Look, your King!" (19:14, NASB).

The depth to which the religious leaders had sunk surfaces now as they shout back at Pilate, "We have no king but Caesar" (19:15, KJV). Their hatred of Roman rule was no secret, and Pilate must have been amazed at their duplicity. They had always proclaimed that God was their only king, but now in the heat of this dark moment they had made their choice—it was the kingship of Caesar rather than the Kingdom of God. And in making this choice they had rejected the King of kings.

Matthew tells us that even as the mob was demanding Jesus's death, Pilate called for a basin of water and washed his hands in front of the crowd as a symbol that he was not responsible for the death of an innocent man, but in their madness the crowd accepted that responsibility with their shouts of "Crucify him!" They chose the way of Barabbas and rejected the way of Jesus.

It is easy for us to be critical of the mob that condemned Jesus. We're too civilized to condone a barbarous act of crucifixion and murder. And yet we so often stand aside and compromise the truth. But this same Jesus stands by in love and waits for us to confess Him as Lord (Romans 10:9–10).

Love—that Bears Our Sins

Crucifixion is the most horrible death conceivable. Originally a Persian method, it was taken up by the Romans as a way of executing criminals. The public display of the agony of a person crucified may have been seen as a deterrent to other criminals. The victim was typically nailed (though sometimes tied) to the cross by spikes driven through the base of the hands. The weight of the body would then cause the victim to sag until the lungs collapsed. And finally, fighting for breath, the dying person would press down on his feet in an effort to straighten up in a struggle for air. For many death came slowly, and the torture dragged on for hours.

Jesus was put to death in this cruel way. Peter wrote, "He himself bore our sins in his body on the tree, that we might die to sin and live to righteousness. By his wounds you have been healed" (1 Peter 2:24, ESV). Jesus literally carried in Himself the full weight of our sin, absorbing our hostility to the death, while at the same time assuring us of forgiveness.

It was customary to have the condemned man carry his own cross (19:17). Weakened and lacerated from the scourging, the victim would stumble along the way, goaded on by the soldiers. One soldier would usually walk ahead of the condemned person carrying a placard naming the offense. In the case of Jesus the sign read "Jesus of Nazareth, the king of the Jews" (19:19, ESV).

Jesus was crucified at Golgotha, the place of the skull, evidently a small hill outside the city wall that was shaped something like a skull. It was near the city, and as people passed by, they could read the inscription, written in Hebrew, Greek, and Latin (19:20). The chief priests asked Pilate to change the wording, but he refused. On this Pilate stood firm.

It was customary also for the soldiers who were on duty at an execution to divide among themselves the few things the crucified person owned. Traditionally, these consisted of five articles: shoes, turban, girdle, tunic, and an outer robe. John tells us that Jesus's tunic was a seamless robe and that the soldiers threw dice to see which one would get it (19:24).

John also refers to the action of the soldiers as being in fulfillment of the prophecy in Psalm 22:18: "They part my garments among them, and cast lots upon my vesture" (KJV).

Love—that Gives Its Life

Crucifixion allowed the dying Savior to communicate words that a sudden death would have prevented. John himself was near the Cross (19:26), witnessing the sordid event. And there were four women standing near the Cross, including Jesus's mother, Mary. Imagine, if you can, how Mary must have felt as she followed Jesus to His death and remembered all of God's promises to her about her son. Also present was Jesus's aunt, Salome, Mary the wife of Clopas, and Mary of Magdala, whom he had delivered from demonic powers (19:25). The faithfulness of these women is a testimony to the meaningful relationships Jesus had with them throughout His ministry (Luke 8:2–3).

John includes the tender scene in which Jesus, in the midst of His agony, attended to the needs of His mother. He commissioned John to become a son in His place and care for Mary, and He called Mary's attention to the new relationship: "Woman, here is your son" (19:26, NIV)—a statement that assured her of John's care. The use of the impersonal-sounding address "Woman" to His mother sounds cold to our modern ears, but most Bible scholars do not interpret it that way. They emphasize the care He demonstrated, even on the Cross, that her needs would be met.

We are told next in verse 28 that Jesus knew that everything had been accomplished, and then He cried, "I am thirsty" (NIV). What is implied here? First, thirst meant that the agony of the Cross was genuine, for intense thirst accompanied crucifixion. Second, Jesus did not think of His own need, His thirst, until after He knew that His atoning work was completed. The reference to giving Jesus vinegar on a sponge affixed to a hyssop branch (19:29) reminds us of the first Passover in Egypt when hyssop was used to put blood on the doorposts and on the lintel as a sign of their deliverance.

John then records Jesus's death cry as a shout of victory: "It is finished" (19:30). The Greek word that is the basis of our English translation is *tetelestai*. It was a cry of victory or achievement. Soldiers used it when they took a city, herdsmen used it when they saw the results of careful animal husbandry, and artists used it when they'd completed a painting. Salvation was now finished. Jesus had faced all of Satan's antagonism and temptations, and He was victor. Satan's opposition was carried to the ultimate, to Jesus's death, but while they crushed Jesus's body, they couldn't crush His spirit!

John makes it clear that Jesus died. "He bowed His head and gave up His spirit" (19:30, NASB). This was in turn attested to by the soldiers who came to break the legs of the men on the crosses—a strategy to quicken death because it kept the victims from pushing up to get their breath. The soldiers didn't break Jesus's legs because they saw He was already dead. He had given His life! One of the soldiers took his lance and pierced Jesus's side, puncturing the heart area. John says that water and blood flowed out. The water mingled with the blood was an indication of the intense suffering He endured at His death.

Socrates wrote to Plato, "It may be that God can forgive sins, but I do not see how." The Good News of the gospel is that Jesus forgives at the deepest cost to Himself. He died in my place, in our place. Calvary reveals the intensity of our sin against Him. But Calvary also expresses the depth of His love for us. We have redemption through His blood.

Love—that Died for Us All

The Apostle's Creed states, "He was crucified, dead, and buried." The account of Jesus's burial is witness to the fact that He actually died (19:38–42). From the time of the Gnostics to today, there have been those who question whether Jesus—as the Son of God—could actually die. Attempts have been made to distinguish between spirit and body in an effort to say that the divine in Jesus of Nazareth could not die. But the Incarnation, as presented in Scripture, tells us of Jesus the Christ who died for us. Paul, writing to the Philippian Christians, said that this Jesus, "who, though he was in the form of God . . . emptied himself . . . being born in the likeness of men. And being found in human form, he humbled himself by becoming obedient to the point of death, even death on a cross" (Philippians 2:6–8, ESV).

Next, in describing Jesus's burial, John tells us that two men were involved: Joseph of Arimathea and Nicodemus. Both men were dissenting members of the Sanhedrin that had condemned Jesus to death (19:38–39). They were also secret disciples of Jesus. Before His death they had kept their belief with modest reserve, but upon His death they came forward to render a special service to Him in a fitting Jewish burial. Joseph provided his own tomb, and Nicodemus brought the spices and linen cloths to shroud the corpse.

As we review the story, it would seem that supporting Jesus in life would have been a better expression of faith than serving Him after death. Yet we applaud their gracious act. And we may conclude that the impact of Jesus's death had a greater influence upon them than had His life.

Unlike the accounts in the three Synoptic gospels, John's account tells us that the day of crucifixion was also the day of preparation for the special Sabbath, special in its association with the Passover. For centuries, Bible scholars have tried to reconcile this apparent difference in timing. John's account states that at the very time the priest was sacrificing the Passover lamb, the Lamb of God died on the Cross! And as evening approached, it was important that, per Jewish law, the body should be taken down and buried before sabbath began at sunset. Joseph and Nicodemus completed this rite as they placed Him in a "a new tomb in which no one had yet been laid" (19:41, NASB).

The descent from the Cross has been the theme of innumerable paintings by artists of many cultures, and it was the theme of Michaelangelo's magnificent *Pietàs*. Among these is one lesser known than the famous *Pietà* in Rome. It is the *Pietà* in Florence in which Nicodemus, rather than Mary, is holding the body of Christ, and Michaelangelo placed his own face on Nicodemus. This witness by the artist calls us to identify with Christ in His death, for with Paul we must say, "I have been crucified with Christ and I no longer live, but Christ lives in me. The life I now live in the body, I live by faith in the Son of God, who loved me and gave himself for me" (Galatians 2:20, NIV).

Abba, Father, help me to daily appreciate my new life in You. I'm sometimes tempted to take it for granted. Give me a fresh vision of Calvary. AMEN.

INSPIRATION FROM THE GOSPEL OF JOHN

When Jesus saw his mother there, and the disciple whom he loved standing nearby, he said to her, "Woman, here is your son," and to the disciple, "Here is your mother." From that time on, this disciple took her into his home.

—John 19:26–27 (NIV)

Of all the verses that depict Jesus's deep, profound, and tender love for us, this one has always felt the most poignant to me. He was in excruciating pain, beaten, bleeding, hanging on a Cross, bearing the sins of the entire world. Yet as He struggled for breath, He took time to assure the future care of His mother.

When I'm in pain, I rarely muster much interest in those around me. It doesn't take hanging on a cross. To be honest, even a simple headache can make me cranky toward everyone in my path. I don't spare any extra energy to think about their needs. It's all about me.

So the way that Jesus showed care for His mother in this moment when He was fulfilling His purpose on earth seems particularly comforting. His words show me His love, but something else as well. His compassion was eminently practical. He made sure she had a home, someone to provide for her.

There are times when I hesitate to bring my day-to-day concerns to Jesus. Surely with all the huge problems in the world, and in the lives of those I know, He has bigger needs to answer than a broken car, a remodeling project gone awry, or a decision about where to live. But then I remember that at the most painful and crucial moments of His mission on earth, He cared about His mother's welfare and tangible needs. He cares for us as well.

—*Sharon Hinck*

Notes

Notes

Notes

LESSON 8: JOHN 20-21

Christ the Reconciler— in Hope

Father, Your Word admonishes me to "glory in understanding and knowing You." Use this lesson to further my knowledge of You, Lord. AMEN.

The resurrection of Jesus is the pivotal point of Christian faith. While the triumph of Jesus was on the Cross, without the empty tomb the victory of the Cross could have been fruitless. Paul summed it up for the Roman Christians by writing that Jesus "was delivered over to death for our sins and was raised to life for our justification" (Romans 4:25, NIV). It is in His life that we live. His resurrection victory is our hope, and hope is acting in faith that His victory is timeless.

Hope—in the Empty Tomb

The other Gospels tell us that Mary Magdalene and several other women came early to the tomb the first day of the week, intending to complete the burial treatment of the body to fulfill Jewish embalming rites. John refers only to Mary, who went very early to the tomb while it was still dark and found to her surprise that the stone was rolled away (20:1). John then adds that Mary ran immediately to the city and reported to Peter and "the other disciple whom Jesus loved"—John himself—that "'they have taken the Lord from the tomb, and we do not know where they have put Him'" (20:2, NASB).

Upon receiving that shocking news, the two men ran to the garden to investigate Mary's story. The younger John outran Peter, and when he arrived at the tomb he stood at the door looking in. But when Peter came up, he went right into the tomb and then John followed. They saw the linen clothes lying neatly in the grave, and the napkin that had been used to wrap Jesus's head, perhaps binding the lower jaw, was folded in place separate from the shroud (20:3–7).

John then testifies to the fact that when he saw the empty shroud in the deserted sepulcher, he became a believer in the resurrection of our Lord (20:8). Even with all that Jesus had said about His death and resurrection on earlier occasions, the disciples still didn't understand. So we have to ask: What did John believe at this point? It is difficult to say, but it must have been the dawning of faith. And yet John now tells us that the two men left that awesome scene and "the disciples went back to their homes" (20:10, ESV). That sounds pretty routine and matter-of-fact. There didn't appear to be any of the resurrection joy and zeal that later turned them into bold witnesses. Evidently the empty grave wasn't enough; they had to meet the risen Lord.

Faith by its very nature is a response to evidence, and these disciples now needed to process the evidence. At the same time we, too, need to look at the evidence. The tomb is empty, the Lord is not there; He is risen. But we today have the benefit of more than 2,000 years of Christian witness: The changed lives of hundreds of thousands of people who have met the risen Christ in faith are evidence that the Lord is active in our world. We need to acknowledge Him, open ourselves to His presence, and realize that we are never alone. Jesus is with us—now!

Hope—in the Risen One

The first person to see the risen Christ was Mary Magdalene (20:11-18). This is one of the most moving stories of the Bible. Mary had come early to the tomb, and as we have just read, when she saw that the stone had been pushed aside, she ran to tell Peter and John.

Apparently Mary returned to the tomb and arrived there after Peter and John had left. After grieving for her lost Lord for a time outside the tomb, she stooped down and looked inside (20:11). It was then that she saw the two angels who asked why she was crying. After explaining her great sense of loss, she turned back into the garden, and through her tears she saw a man standing there whom she presumed was the gardener. In desperation she asked, "Sir, if you have carried him away, tell me where you have put him, and I will get him" (20:15, NIV).

The next moment presents the greatest scene of recognition in the resurrection stories. The man standing there, Jesus Himself, spoke her name, "Mary," in a tone that she immediately recognized. She cried out, "Rabboni!" an Aramaic word that recognizes the divine in the teacher. It was as though

Mary cried out, "My Lord!" This was her great confession as she fell at His feet (20:16).

Evidently Mary grasped Jesus's feet, for He said, "Do not cling to me, for I have not yet ascended to the Father" (20:17, ESV). Again Jesus was referring to the coming event mentioned earlier in His prayer (chapter 17) when He was preparing the disciples for His return to the Father. Now He was telling Mary the same thing, and then He added, "Go to my brothers and say to them, 'I am ascending to my Father and your Father, to my God and your God'" (20:17, ESV). What a powerful message of reconciliation and hope for the questioning and confused disciples—and for us. Through Jesus, His Father and His God is *our* Father and *our* God.

Mary now became the first witness of the Resurrection. Since it came from her and not one of Jesus's disciples, this may be seen as adding credibility to the witness. It can also be seen as Jesus's confirmation of the importance of women, as well as men, among His disciples. Mary then ran to tell the disciples that she had seen the Lord and talked with Him. Now it was not only the empty tomb that Peter and John had as evidence of Jesus's resurrection but also the witness of one who had seen Jesus and knew beyond a doubt that He was alive—He is risen!

Hope—in Peace for All

The post-Resurrection appearances of Jesus are variously reported by the Gospel writers. John includes several accounts not reported in the other three Gospels, even as the others describe some that John omits. We are told by Luke of

Jesus's appearance to two people as they walked on the road to Emmaus. After these two discovered who their fellow traveler really was, they hurried back and learned from their friends that Jesus was alive and had appeared to Peter. It was later that evening that Jesus appeared to the disciples—the story John now tells us (20:19–23).

John writes that the disciples were behind closed doors for fear of the Jewish leaders. How often our fears cause us to withdraw, to hide behind our masks, to seek protection in our limited securities. We next read that suddenly Jesus stood among them and said, "Peace be unto you" (20:19, KJV)—*Shalom* in Hebrew. This is the abiding greeting of God's grace. It was a common greeting in Jesus's day, and it has also lived through the centuries to the present time.

Jesus followed the greeting by showing the disciples His hands and His side (20:20). These were the three main wounds from the Cross and were the evidence that they were really seeing their crucified and risen Lord. The joy of the disciples was the expression of their dawning faith. Again Jesus said, "Peace be unto you" (20:21, KJV).

The next phrase, "As the Father has sent me, I am sending you" (verse 21, NIV), reminds us of the great commission and is almost a direct quotation from His prayer in John 17:18. Jesus was sending His disciples out into a ministry of reconciliation, a ministry of the same nature as His own reconciling ministry.

Dr. E. Stanley Jones, missionary-statesman to India, told the story of a visit with Mahatma Ghandi in which he asked, "What should I do? I am an American Christian missionary;

do you want me to go home?" Ghandi replied, "No, but live your religion, be clear about what you believe, make love primary, and be more understanding of other religions." This is a great four-point mission strategy as we carry out Jesus's commission in today's world.

In verse 22 we are given what seems like a pre-Pentecost Pentecost when Jesus said, "Receive the Holy Spirit" (ESV). However, the problem of relating this to the event in Acts 2 can be resolved by noting that the Greek language here is imperative, a command. It could well read, "You *must* receive the Holy Spirit." And while this particular account in John gives no further explanation, we can readily conclude that Jesus's command became a reality several weeks later on the Day of Pentecost. John's reporting of this command of Jesus corresponds to the instructions in Luke 24:49, where the disciples were told by Jesus to stay in Jerusalem until they received the Holy Spirit.

Jesus then closed this dialogue with the disciples by declaring that the privilege of telling people that their sins are forgiven, or the responsibility to hold the unrepentant accountable, is a work of the Holy Spirit (20:23). We can serve God in this way only when we are operating in His presence under the anointing of the Spirit.

Hope—in Answers to Doubt

The expression "a doubting Thomas" is familiar to many people and is used frequently to describe someone who is a skeptic. It is from the story John tells us now that this expression comes (20:24–31). But perhaps we've been unfair in labeling Thomas this way. As a careful and logical thinker, he may simply have been asking for evidence.

Another common expression is "Seeing is believing." Here we read that Thomas, the twin (thought by some to have been the twin of Matthew), was not present that first evening when Jesus appeared. When he was told that the risen Lord had visited with the disciples and had showed them His hands and His side, Thomas made what seems to be a normal response, "Unless I see . . . I will never believe" (20:25, ESV). But we also read that "seeing" wasn't going to be quite enough, for Thomas said that he would believe when he could put his finger into the print of the nails and his hand into the wound in Jesus's side. It is the intensity and detail of his statement that indicate the extent to which Thomas needed to be convinced.

John then describes a scene eight days later when the disciples, including Thomas, were together once again and suddenly, without warning, Jesus came into the room through closed doors and greeted them with the same word: "Peace."

This time Jesus centered His attention on Thomas and picked up on Thomas's words of a week before when He said, "Put your finger here; see my hands. Reach out your hand and put it into my side" (20:27, NIV). And then Jesus told him, "Do not be unbelieving, but [stop doubting and] believe" (verse 27, AMP).

Jesus's response to Thomas called for him to recognize that the highest form of faith is not tied to the senses but is related to evidence in other forms (20:29). Thomas responded with his great confession of faith, "My Lord and my God!"

(20:28, NIV). He moved from unfaith to faith—the most that can occur in a person.

Before moving on, here are a few observations on doubt. First, doubt is the normal function of the seeking and inquiring mind. As Christians, it is normal to doubt, to ask questions, to seek certainty. Second, doubt is as much a matter of the heart or will as of the mind. The real issues are, do we want to know God, and do we want God in our lives? Dr. A. T. Robertson, prominent New Testament scholar of the early 20th century, used to say that doubt is not necessarily a mark of intellectual superiority. And third, when the evidence is clear, doubt, when honest, becomes as thoroughly convinced as it was when questioning.

John has written this Gospel as evidence (20:31). He selected from Jesus's life and ministry those words and events he was led to write with the specific purpose that we "might believe that Jesus is the Christ, the Son of God," and that in so believing we "might have life through his name" (20:31, KJV).

Hope—in Evidence of His Presence

Jesus had told His disciples that after the Resurrection He would meet them in Galilee (Matthew 26:32; Mark 16:7). Then to make certain they understood, the angel in the empty tomb on Resurrection morning told "Mary Magdalene and the other Mary" to tell the disciples that He would meet them at the mountain in Galilee that He had designated. We may surmise that in their uncertainty about Jesus's resurrection they didn't leave at once because the first two appearances Jesus made to the disciples, which we have just studied, occurred in Jerusalem. We don't know the reason for the delay—it may have been travel plans or possibly Thomas had been away from Jerusalem for a few days. But whatever the cause, after Jesus's second appearance, they left Jerusalem and traveled to Galilee. John now tells us about Jesus's third visit with the disciples (21:1–14).

Peter had no doubt become impatient with sitting around waiting for the unknown and turned to the known, for he announced, "I am going fishing" (21:3, NASB). Six other disciples responded and went with him. In a pattern well understood by such veteran Galilean fishermen, they spent the night on the lake but with no success.

As the mist was lifting at early dawn, the figure of a man could be seen on the shore. The man asked if they had any fish, and they admitted their failure (21:5). Then the man called back and said, "Cast the net on the right side of the boat, and you will find some" (21:6, ESV). Still not recognizing Jesus, they did what He said because it was not unusual for a person standing on the shore to see a school of fish not visible at the moment to men in a boat. The result was staggering. The nets were so full they weren't able of themselves to pull them in (21:6).

John then turned to Peter with the awareness of faith. "It is the Lord," he said (21:7, KJV). Peter, stripped to his loincloth, grabbed his cloak and plunged into the water, hurrying to the shore to greet his Lord. When the other disciples arrived on shore, they discovered that Jesus had built a fire and cooked some fish for their breakfast. Then at a word from Jesus, Peter pulled up the net and added fish to the fire from their catch.

John now tells us that while they were eating the fish and bread Jesus had prepared for them, "None of the disciples dared ask him, 'Who are you?' They knew it was the Lord" (21:12, NIV). The act of eating with them was a certification of His person and a renewal of their relationship.

This story of the third appearance of the risen Christ to a group of the disciples demonstrates the reality of the Resurrection. While some people might want to believe that Jesus's appearances in the room in Jerusalem were hallucinations or visions from the spirit world, this story points to the truth that the risen Christ was a real person, not a spirit or vision. The risen Christ acted and talked like the Jesus of Nazareth they had lived with for over three years. He ate with them in familiar fellowship. He made it clear that He was the same Jesus, risen from the grave, conqueror of death!

Belief in the bodily resurrection of Jesus Christ was the transforming faith that changed the disciples. When we meet them in the ministries recorded in the book of Acts, they are boldly announcing the resurrection of Jesus and His reign as Lord of lords.

Hope—in the Testing of Our Love

Following breakfast that morning Jesus turned to Peter for a personal conversation (21:15–19). He had met Peter earlier to assure him of His love and forgiveness. But now, this personal interview with Peter in the presence of the other disciples reinstated him with the group and recommissioned him for service.

Peter had denied his Lord three times, and now Jesus asked him three times about his love (21:15–17). In telling the story, John uses two different Greek words that in English are translated "love." Because of this, it is easy to miss the play on words that is taking place in this exchange, as the difference between the two words is very significant. In Jesus's questions He used the word *agape* (uh-GAH-peh)—self-giving love. When Peter responded, he used the word *phileo* (fill-EH-o)—friendship love.

First, Jesus asked, "Simon son of John, do you love me more than these?" (21:15, NIV). The reference may have been to the fishing boats anchored nearby. We can't tell because we have no way of knowing what objects Jesus gestured toward. If so, He was calling Peter to a vocation that transcended occupation. On the other hand, the reference may have been to the other disciples, for Peter had said earlier that even though everyone else might desert Him, he wouldn't. If that was the case, Jesus was leading Peter to take his place with the other disciples—all of whom were dependent upon God's grace. Peter's answer was that he had great friendship-love for Jesus.

Next, Jesus asked, "Simon son of John, do you love me?" (21:16, NIV). Again, Jesus used the word *agape*. This time Jesus may have been pressing the issue of the nature of Peter's love. Or the question may have been focusing on the object of his love—do you love *Me*? It may be that Jesus wanted Peter to see the difference between loving Him and loving himself. Again, Peter responded by using *phileo*: You know that I am Your friend.

The third time Jesus asked the question He used Peter's word *phileo* and asked, in essence, "Are you truly my friend?" (See 21:17.) John writes that Peter was grieved over the third question, either because of Jesus's repeated questioning or perhaps because Jesus now raised the question about his "friendship-love." Clearly Jesus pressed Peter to the point of full honesty, of full self-awareness. For then Peter burst out, "Lord, you know everything; you know that I love you" (21:17, ESV).

To each of Peter's answers Jesus responded with a commission: "Feed my lambs," "Tend my sheep," and, "Feed my sheep" (21:15–17, ESV). We may conclude that the evidence of Peter's love would be his service in the vocation to which Christ was calling him—shepherding the church that would soon emerge. Love involves responsibility. Love means faithfulness. But it also means active service at the cost of one's self. And loving service is a necessary corollary to loving proclamation. Social concern and evangelistic proclamation belong together. We cannot separate faith from works, verbal witness from action.

Jesus closed this dialogue with Peter by predicting Peter's future martyrdom. And then He added one more time, "Follow me" (21:19, KJV). This Peter did, and as shepherd of the church, he later referred in his writings to his role and that of his colleagues—and us—as "under shepherds" awaiting the appearance of the "Chief Shepherd" (1 Peter 5:2–4).

Hope—in the Testimony of His Word

In these closing words (21:20–25) we get a clue that John, the writer of this Gospel, must have written with the help of others. The witness to the truth of his testimony (21:24) was no doubt made by those in Ephesus who assisted him in his writing.

After hearing what Jesus said about his future (21:18), Peter looked around and, seeing John nearby, asked, "Lord, and what about this man?" (21:21, NASB). In Jesus's response He seems to be saying that it doesn't matter what happens to John or anyone else. Instead, it was important for Peter to remain faithful and in submission to his Master.

The wording of Jesus's response, "If I want him to remain until I come, what is that to you?" was evidently interpreted by some to mean that John would not die. John corrects this misapprehension by telling us what Jesus actually said (21:23, NASB). John wanted to be sure that the record was set straight.

But the important thing to note in verse 22 is the words "till I come" (KJV). The promise of His second coming is simple and direct just as it had been throughout all of His teaching ministry. It is only His later interpreters that have added complexities to this great truth.

Now, as John comes to the end of his Gospel (21:25), having selected words and events from Christ's life, death, and resurrection to express the "Good News," he seems reluctant to conclude. His closing statement is witness to the greatness of our Lord and the extent of His revelation. John says that if everything Jesus did was recorded, "I suppose that the world itself could not contain the books that would be written" (ESV). Actually, John is expressing his faith in the limitless meaning of the knowledge of God in Jesus Christ.

The story is told of William Whiting Borden, who turned his back on a huge family fortune to follow his call to go to China as a missionary. He got as far as Egypt, where he contracted typhoid fever and died, a young man still in his twenties. His dedication to the Lord was expressed in these words in a 1927 biography about Borden, "No reserve, no retreat, and no regret." It is this indomitable spirit—the spirit of Peter and John, the Gospel writer—that has opened up the testimony of God's Word in all time. John expressed it so well in the opening verses of the Gospel: "to all who did receive him, to those who believed in his name, he gave the right to become children of God" (1:12, NIV). This is the Good News of the gospel for everyone in all time. Our hope is in Jesus Christ—our mission is to live that hope so that people everywhere are drawn to the Savior.

Lord God, help me to "live that hope"—Your hope—that frees me to rejoice and be confident in You! AMEN.

INSPIRATION FROM THE GOSPEL OF JOHN

He said to them, "Cast the net on the right-hand side of the boat, and you will find the fish." So they cast it, and then they were not able to haul it in because of the great quantity of fish.

—John 21:6 (NASB)

Many curiosities lace the life Jesus lived on earth. One of the incidents happened the day several disciples turned their uncertainty into a fishing trip. Their Master, Jesus, had suffered a cruel death on a cross, had been buried for three days, had risen to life again, and had appeared to them with the announcement that He was soon to leave them again.

What were they to do with that information? They went fishing. They'd fished all night with their nets on the port side of the boat. All night. Nothing. Although they didn't recognize who He was, in the morning a man on the shore called out to them, asking if they'd caught anything. The Man said, "Cast your net on the right side of the boat, and you will find some."

The distance between the port and starboard sides of the boat couldn't have been more than a few feet. For reasons unknown to us, the expert fishermen obeyed the stranger's advice and cast their nets on the opposite side. The haul of fish was so great, they struggled to drag them all to shore. Was the story told to log yet another miracle in the journal of the life of Jesus? Or is there an application for us?

"Cast your net on the other side" speaks to my heart. Sometimes I miss the right thing, but not by much. What I perceive as failure could be a misjudgment by a few feet. Solution? Listen carefully to the direction Jesus gives me, whether it seems to make sense or not.

—*Cynthia Ruchti*

Notes

Notes

Notes

Appendix

The Specific Miracles of Jesus in the Gospel of John

Jesus turns the water into wine at the wedding at Cana. 2:1–11
Jesus heals the nobleman's son. 4:46–54
Jesus heals the man at the Pool of Bethesda. 5:1–16
The feeding of the 5,000. 6:1–14
Jesus walks on the Sea of Galilee. 6:15–21
Jesus heals the man born blind. 9:1–41
Lazarus is raised from the dead. 11:1–44

The "I Am" Statements in the Gospel of John

Unique to the Gospel of John are seven "I am" statements that Jesus made. By including these simple yet powerful statements throughout the book, the writer identifies Jesus with Yahweh, the great I Am whom Moses encountered in the burning bush (see Exodus 3:14) and establishes His divinity. Together with the miracles and signs of Jesus recorded throughout the book, they make the case for the theme of John's Gospel, "that Jesus is the Messiah, the Son of God" (20:31, NIV), so that we might have life in His name.

1. I am the bread of life. 6:35
2. I am the light of the world. 8:12
3. I am the door. 10:7
4. I am the good shepherd. 10:11
5. I am the resurrection and the life. 11:25
6. I am the way, the truth, and the life. 14:6
7. I am the true vine. 15:1

Map of Jesus's Travels in the Gospel of John

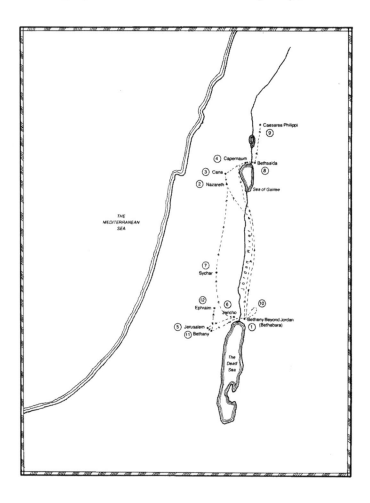

Jesus's Travels in the Gospel of John

When we read about the life of Jesus, it doesn't take long to discover that He rarely stayed in one place for very long. As He famously said about Himself in Luke 9:58 (NIV), "Foxes have dens and birds have nests, but the Son of Man has no place to lay his head." Starting from the earliest days of His itinerant preaching ministry, Jesus made frequent journeys.

Jesus primarily stayed in Galilee, and most of the events of the Gospels took place in an area of around 3,000 square miles (approximately twice the size of Rhode Island). Though this area seems small in our era of rapid transit, it is important to remember that He was traveling on foot, as was the norm for most people in His time, and covering even this relatively small territory would have been time-consuming and tiring.

Though the territory Jesus covered in the four Gospels is well known and documented, scholars can only make educated guesses about the linear distance He traveled. Some experts suggest that He traveled an average of 20 miles per day. By some estimates, Jesus traveled around 3,000 miles during His three years of teaching, and as many as 21,000 miles during His earthly lifetime. To give us some perspective on the breadth of his journeys, it is helpful to know that the distance between Jerusalem and Nazareth is 85 to 91 miles.

When we look at it in this way, it becomes plain that traveling played a large part in fulfilling His purpose and mission when He lived among us here on earth. Following is a chronological overview from John's Gospel of Jesus's travels during the three years in which He was active in His ministry. You'll be able to follow Jesus's travels on the map provided on page 202 by using the numbers next to place names in the text below.

The Gospel of John places Jesus at the beginning of His ministry at Bethany beyond Jordan ① but, undoubtedly, as Matthew and Mark indicate, Jesus had traveled there from Nazareth, the town where Jesus grew up, ② by taking the route just east of the Jordan River. It is here that Jesus was baptized by John the Baptist (John 1:19–34). While the Gospel writer John does not give us the story of Jesus's temptation in the Judean wilderness, he does give us the account of Jesus's first encounter with Andrew, Peter, Philip, and Nathanael, who were early followers of John the Baptist (John 1:35–51).

From there, Jesus traveled north and west to attend the wedding at Cana, ③ just a few miles north of Nazareth ② (John 2:1–11). There, during the seven days of the wedding feast, Jesus, in response to need, turned the water at the wedding feast into superior-quality wine. At the conclusion of the wedding feast, Jesus traveled to Capernaum, ④ a fishing town on the north shore of the Sea of Galilee (John 2:12).

Jesus headed south briefly on His Passover trip to Jerusalem ⑤ (John 2:13). It was at this time, according to John, that He drove the money changers out of the Temple and had His conversation with Nicodemus (John 2:14–3:21). Next we find Jesus and His disciples leaving Judea, possibly from Jericho ⑥, and heading northwest through Samaria, where He met the Samaritan woman at the well of Jacob in

Sychar ⑦ (John 4:5–38). They stayed on in Sychar for two days, preaching and teaching, and many of the Samaritans came to believe in Jesus during that time (John 4:39–42).

Upon leaving Sychar ⑦ they continued north through Nazareth ② to Cana ③. Word had apparently spread as far as Capernaum ④ that Jesus was in Cana, ③ because we read that a Capernaum official, upon learning where Jesus was, found Him and begged Him to heal his son, who was at home, desperately ill. Jesus responded, not by going to Capernaum ④ at that moment but by assuring the official that his son was healed and would live (John 4:46–53).

In all probability, Jesus later went on to Capernaum, ④ but then He again traveled south, quite likely on either the route just west of the Jordan River or the eastside route, to Jerusalem, ⑤ where He healed the disabled man at the Pool of Bethesda (John 5:1–18).

John 6:1–15 places Jesus and His disciples back in Galilee, probably returning there from Jerusalem ⑤ by way of either the east or west route along the Jordan River. Out from Bethsaida ⑧ Jesus fed the 5,000 with the five barley loaves and two fish.

From the region of Bethsaida, ⑧ the disciples took a boat and traveled the short distance across the northern tip of the Sea of Galilee toward Capernaum ④. John tells us that it was during this crossing that Jesus appeared to the disciples while walking on the rough sea (John 6:16–21).

John 6:26–66 shows us Jesus teaching in the synagogue at Capernaum, ④ after which, while John's account does not so indicate, they traveled north to Caesarea Philippi, ⑨ where

Peter gave his great confession of faith (John 6:67–71). After returning to Capernaum, ④ Jesus stayed there until it was time for Him once again to head south to Jerusalem. ⑤

In John 7:1–10:39 Jesus taught and healed the sick in the region around Jerusalem. ⑤ Then when the authorities attempted once again to kill Him, He retreated to an undefined region east of the Jordan River ⑩ (John 10:40–42) where he remained until He received word of Lazarus's death (John 11:1–6). Moving west across the Jordan River, Jesus and His disciples made their way to Bethany, ⑪ where he raised Lazarus from the dead (John 11:7–44).

The act of restoring life to Lazarus and its impact on the crowds polarized the Jewish authorities, and they determined that Jesus must die (John 11:45–53). It was this threat that caused Jesus to take His disciples to the secluded town of Ephraim, ⑫ probably 10–15 miles north of Bethany (John 11:54). ⑪

Six days before the Passover they returned to Bethany (John 12:1–11), ⑪ and on what we know now as Palm Sunday, Jesus went to Jerusalem. ⑤ From John 12:20–19:42 we read about Jesus's actions and teachings through what we observe as Holy Week, culminating in His arrest and trial and crucifixion.

In the grand finale of John's Gospel, 20:1–10, we read of Christ's resurrection, and from John 20:11–30 Jesus shows Himself to Mary in the garden and to His disciples, who report, "We have seen the Lord."

The Palestine of Jesus's Time

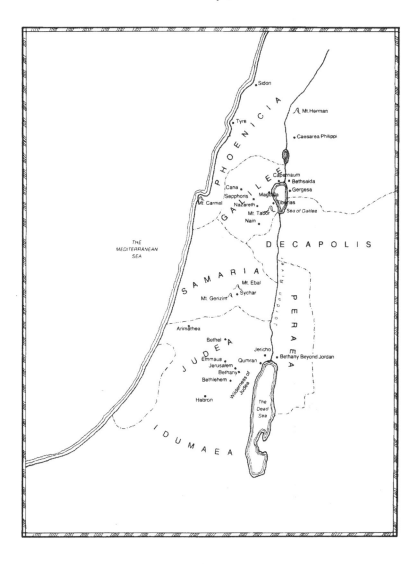

APPENDIX 207

Map of the Jerusalem/Jericho Region

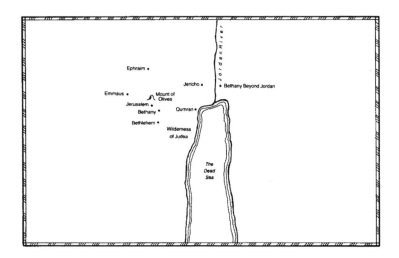

Map of the Region around the Sea of Galilee

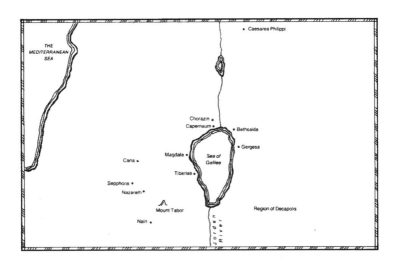

APPENDIX

A Harmony of the Gospels

The Gospel of John is different from the other New Testament Gospels, which are collectively called the Synoptic Gospels. While Matthew, Mark, and Luke are similar in their telling of the events of Jesus's life and ministry on earth, John includes some unique accounts that are missing in the other Gospels, while omitting or reordering some of the accounts included in the others. The first harmony of the first four books of the New Testament was written by St. Augustine in the fifth century AD. A harmony of the Gospels is an educated attempt to bring the four accounts into a more or less sequential, chronological order that includes virtually all of the stories of Jesus in the New Testament. We have included one here.

	MATTHEW	MARK	LUKE	JOHN
The genealogy of Jesus	1:1–17		3:23–38	
The birth of John the Baptist			1:5–25; 57–80	
The birth of Jesus	1:5–25; 2:1		2:1–20	
The wise men find Jesus	2:1–12			
The Flight to Egypt	2:13–23			
The boy Jesus at the temple			2:41–50	
John the Baptist preaches and baptizes	3:1–12	1:1–8	3:1–20	
Jesus's baptism	3:13–17	1:9–11	3:21–22	
Jesus's temptation	4:1–11	1:12–13	4:1–13	
Jesus's first miracle at Cana				2:1–11
Jesus and Nicodemus				3:1–21
Jesus and the Samaritan woman				4:5–42
Jesus heals the nobleman's son				4:46–54
Jesus selects four disciples	4:18–22	1:16–20	5:1–11	
Demon-possessed man healed		1:23–28	4:31–37	

Jesus gives the Sermon on the Mount	5:1 – 7:29		6:20–49
The parable of the two builders	7:24–27		6:47–49
Jesus heals a leper	8:1–4	1:40–45	5:12–14
The centurion's servant healed	8:5–13		7:1–10
Peter's mother-in-law healed	8:14–15	1:29–31	4:38–39
Life restored to the widow's son			7:11–17
Jesus calms the storm	8:23–27	4:36–41	8:22–25
Demon-possessed men healed	8:28–34	5:1–21	8:26–40
Paralyzed man healed	9:1–8	2:3–12	5:18–26
Life restored to Jairus's daughter	9:18–19, 23–26	5:22–24, 35–43	8:41–42, 49–56
Woman healed of hemorrhage	9:20–22	5:25–34	8:43–48
Blind man healed (Capernaum)	9:27–31		
Devil cast out of mute man	9:32–34		
The disciples sent on tour	10:1–11:1	6:7–13	9:1–6
Man with withered hand healed	12:9–14	3:1–5	6:6–11
The parable of the sower	13:4–9, 18–23	4:1–20	8:14–15
The parable of the tares	13:24–30		
The parable of the mustard seed	13:31–32	4:30–32	
The parable of the leaven	13:33–34		13:20–21
The parable of hidden treasure	13:44		
The parable of the pearl	13:45		
The parable of the net	13:47–50		
John the Baptist killed	14:1–12	6:14–29	9:7–9

Text continues on following page

APPENDIX 211

	MATTHEW	MARK	LUKE	JOHN
The feeding of the 5,000	14:13–21	6:33–44	9:11–17	6:1–14
Jesus walks on the sea	14:22–33	6:45–52		6:15–21
Canaanite woman's daughter healed	15:21–28	7:24–30		
The feeding of the 4,000	15:32–38	8:1–9		
Blind man at Bethsaida healed		8:22–26		
Peter's great confession	16:13–26	8:27–37	9:18–25	
The transfiguration of Jesus	16:27—17:13	8:38—9:13	9:26–36	
Lunatic boy healed	17:14–21	9:14–29	9:37–43	
Tax money from fish's mouth	17:24–27			
The parable of the wealthy farmer			12:16–21	
Crippled woman healed			13:10–13	
The parable of the lost sheep	18:12–13		15:3–7	
The parable of the lost coin			15:8–10	
The parable of the prodigal son			15:11–32	
The parable of the unmerciful servant	18:23–35			
Jesus and the rich young ruler	19:16—20:16	10:17–31	18:18–30	
The adulterous woman				8:1–11
Man born blind healed				9:1–41
The parable of the good shepherd				10:1–18
The parable of the good Samaritan			10:30–37	
The parable of the friend at midnight			11:5–10	

The parable of the good father			
Lazarus raised from the dead			11:1–44
Jesus heals ten lepers			17:11–19
The parable of the laborers in the vineyard	20:1–16		
Jesus heals the blind men	20:29–34	10:46–52	18:35–43
Jesus and the barren fig tree	21:18–22	11:12–14, 20–26	
The parable of the man with two sons	21:28–32		
Jesus and Zacchaeus			19:1–10
The parable of the landowner	21:33–44	12:1–9	20:9–19
The triumphal entry of Jesus	21:1–11	11:1–10	19:29–40	12:12–19
Jesus clears the temple	21:12–13	11:15–19	19:45–48
The parable of the marriage feast	22:1–14		14:16–24
The parable of the fig tree	24:32	13:28–31	21:29–33
The parable of the virgins	25:1–13		
The parable of the man, his servants, and the talents	25:14–30		
Jesus looks ahead to His Crucifixion	26:1–5	14:1–2	22:1–2
Mary anoints Jesus	26:6–13	14:3–9		12:2–8
Judas plots with authorities	26:14–16	14:10–11	22:3–6
Last Passover and the Lord's Supper	26:20–29	14:17–21	22:7–30
Jesus in Gethsemane	26:36–46	14:32–42	22:39–46	18:1
Betrayal and arrest of Jesus	26:47–56	14:43–52	22:47–53	18:2–12

Text continues on following page

APPENDIX   213

	MATTHEW	MARK	LUKE	JOHN
Jesus's trial before Caiaphas and the Sanhedrin	26:57–68	14:55–65	22:63–65	18:24
Peter denies Jesus	26:69–75	14:66–72	22:54–62	18:15–18
Jesus's trial before Pilate	27:11–26	15:1–15	23:1–25	18:28–40; 19:1–15
The Crucifixion of Jesus	27:33–56	15:22–41	23:33–49	19:16–30
The burial of Jesus	27:57–61	15:42–47	23:50–56	19:38–42
The resurrection of Jesus	28:1–10	16:1–7	24:1–12	20:1–10
Post-Resurrection appearances	28:9–10, 16–20	16:9–18	24:13–48	20:11–29; 21:1–22
The ascension of Jesus		16:19–20	24:50–53	

Notes

Notes

Notes

Notes

Acknowledgments

Every attempt has been made to credit the sources of copyrighted material used in this book. If any such acknowledgment has been inadvertently omitted or miscredited, receipt of such information would be appreciated.

Scripture quotations marked (AMP) are taken from the *Amplified Bible*. Copyright © 2015 by The Lockman Foundation, La Habra, California. All rights reserved.

Scripture quotations marked (ESV) are taken from *The Holy Bible, English Standard Version*. Copyright © 2001 by Crossway Bibles, a division of Good News Publishers. Used by permission. All rights reserved.

Scripture quotations marked (KJV) are taken from the *King James Version of the Bible.*

Scripture quotations marked (NASB) are taken from the *New American Standard Bible*®, Copyright © 1960, 1971, 1977, 1995, 2020 by The Lockman Foundation. All rights reserved.

Scripture quotations marked (NIV) are taken from *The Holy Bible, New International Version*®*, NIV*®. Copyright © 1973, 1978, 1984, 2011 by Biblica, Inc. Used by permission. All rights reserved worldwide.

A Note from the Editors

◆────────────◆

We hope you enjoyed *Living with Purpose Bible Study: John* published by Guideposts. For over 75 years, Guideposts, a nonprofit organization, has been driven by a vision of a world filled with hope. We aspire to be the voice of a trusted friend, a friend who makes you feel more hopeful and connected.

By making a purchase from Guideposts, you join our community in touching millions of lives, inspiring them to believe that all things are possible through faith, hope, and prayer. Your continued support allows us to provide uplifting resources to those in need. Whether through our communities, websites, apps, or publications, we inspire our audiences, bring them together, and comfort, uplift, entertain, and guide them. Visit us at guideposts.org to learn more.

We would love to hear from you. Write us at Guideposts, P.O. Box 5815, Harlan, Iowa 51593 or call us at (800) 932-2145. Did you love *Living with Purpose Bible Study: John*? Leave a review for this product on guideposts.org/shop. Your feedback helps others in our community find relevant products.

Find inspiration, find faith, find Guideposts.
Shop our best sellers and favorites at
guideposts.org/shop
Or scan the QR code to go directly to our Shop

Printed in the United States
by Baker & Taylor Publisher Services